CROCHET at WORK

CROCHET at WORK

20 career dolls to make and customize

Kate McCully

THE GUILD OF MASTER CRAFTSMAN
PUBLICATIONS

Contents

How to use this book

In this book there are 20 fantastic, fully customizable career dolls to crochet, from singers to scientists and dancers to doctors. You can follow the patterns exactly to create the examples in this book, or you can change the doll's body shape or size, skin colour, hairstyle and hair colour to create your own unique doll.

1. CHOOSE THE DOLL
Choose the doll design you want to make (see pages 30–129).

2. CHOOSE THE BODY SHAPE
There are three doll body shapes / sizes to choose from: A, B and C (see pages 16–23). Each individual doll pattern will state which body shape has been used for the example shown, but you can choose whichever you would like to use, as every doll can be made in any body shape.

3. CHOOSE SKIN COLOUR & HAIR COLOUR
The yarn used for these dolls is Ricorumi DK. It comes in a range of wonderful colours (see right), which is great for selecting skin tone and hair colour. The patterns will say what colours have been chosen for the dolls pictured, but you can change them to whatever you would like. For more information on yarn see page 8.

Go to pages 130–131 for some ideas on how to customize the dolls.

4. CHOOSE HAIRSTYLE
There are lots of hairstyles to choose from (see pages 24–29). The hair is crocheted as a cap, then either left like that or is adapted to make the different styles. The head on each body shape pattern is the same size so the hairstyles will fit any doll.

5. MAKE THE DOLL
All the dolls are crocheted in one piece from the feet up, with the colour changes forming their clothes (rather than separate clothing).

Find the body shape you want to make on the individual doll page and follow the pattern referring back to the body shape patterns on pages 16–23 as necessary. Not all the dolls will need all elements of the basic body shape pattern; for example, there is no need to make the ears for the Pilot or Racing driver. So, if an element is not listed in the specific doll pattern, there is no need to make it.

6. MAKE THE ACCESSORIES
All of the dolls have accessories. Patterns for these are provided on the individual project pages.

Skin colours   Hair colours

Tools and materials

To make the crochet dolls in this book you will need a few basic tools and materials. All these items can be readily purchased from a wide variety of suppliers. See page 133 for suggestions on where to source them.

Yarn

The yarn used for most of the dolls is Ricorumi DK (100% cotton, 25g). There is one doll, the Dancer on pages 82–85, that uses a neon version of the Ricorumi that is acrylic rather than cotton, but you can replace the colours with similar shades in cotton if you prefer.

Other yarns can be used to make these dolls, but bear in mind that using an alternative weight of yarn will result in your doll coming out a different size or height. Using an acrylic yarn may also give varied results to shape and size.

All dolls will need only one ball of each colour unless otherwise stated.

Crochet hook

All the dolls in this book use the same yarn so all use the same-sized hook – 2.5mm (US C/2). If you are using a different yarn weight, then you may need to adjust your hook size to suit. The only other time you will require a different size is for attaching hair (see page 25), where a smaller hook is useful – 2mm (US B/1) or smaller.

Stitch markers

Stitch markers are a must when working in the amigurumi style (in a spiral without joining at the end of a round). The start of the round is not obvious, so a marker is inserted into the first stitch of every round. They come in all sorts of shapes and sizes, so pick some that work for you.

Tapestry needle

The dolls are designed in a way to minimize sewing, but a little sewing is required here and there, and also for the accessories. Usually, you will use a tail end of the yarn to sew, so a tapestry needle is ideal as it has a large eye to enable threading the yarn easily. For smaller pieces you will need sewing thread in a similar colour to the yarn you are using. If you don't have any, you can split the yarn into 2–3 strands instead, although this may not be strong enough over a large piece as it tends to break when pulled through a lot.

Scissors or snips

Make sure you have a small, sharp pair to hand.

Pins

For blocking and securing pieces in place before sewing.

Toy stuffing

I use 100% polyester toy stuffing, which can be bought in most craft stores and online. 50g should be plenty of stuffing for one doll.

Safety eyes

All the dolls need a pair of black safety eyes that are approx $5/16$in (7.5mm) in diameter. If you are using different yarn and your doll is a different size, you may need to select different-sized eyes. See Suppliers on page 133 for information on where to purchase the eyes.

Warning: it is not a good idea to use safety eyes if children under the age of three will be playing with the dolls. Embroidered eyes would be more suitable.

Other materials

Some of the dolls will require additional materials, such as sewing thread. They will be stated on the pattern page for that doll.

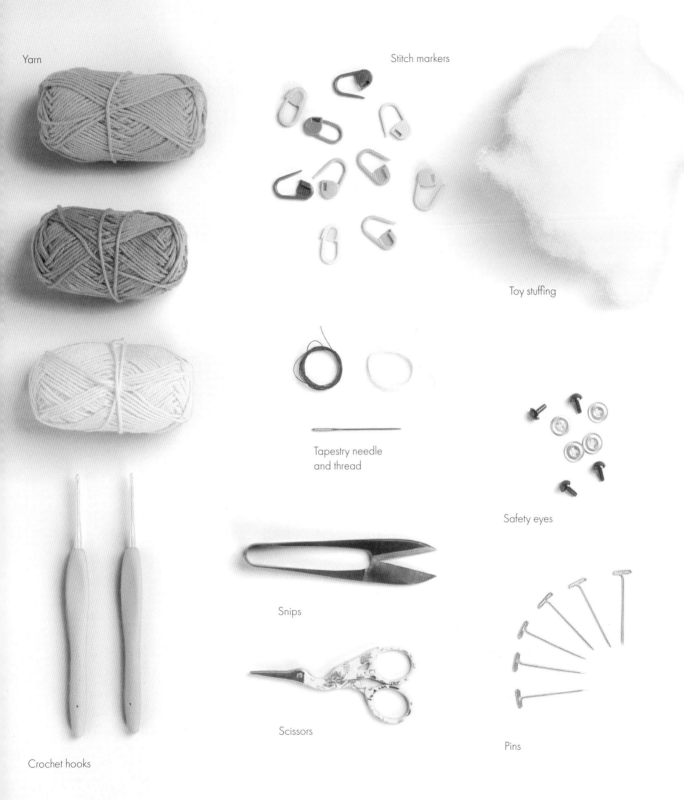

Yarn

Stitch markers

Toy stuffing

Tapestry needle
and thread

Safety eyes

Crochet hooks

Snips

Scissors

Pins

Pattern notes

Before you start, it's a good idea to familiarize yourself with the basic information that applies to all the patterns in this book. This will help you to get the dolls right first time.

Amigurumi

The patterns are worked in the amigurumi style, which is in a spiral without joining at the end of a round. Use a stitch marker or waste yarn to keep track of the first stitch of each round.

Crochet terms

The patterns use UK crochet terms. See page 132 for US terms.

Rounds vs rows

For these dolls you will mostly be crocheting in rounds. The pattern indicates this by stating 'round' at the start of each line instruction. Where you see 'rounds 2–4' for example, you follow the same instructions for all those rounds. Sometimes the patterns will switch to working in rows (the hair cap for example). The pattern will warn you and the word 'row' will be used instead.

Repeats in rounds

If a round repeats a certain set of stitches, the repeat is placed in brackets and then states how many times it is repeated. For example, '(2 dc in next st, 3dc) 6 times' shows the stitch pattern in the bracket is repeated six times.

Right side (RS) vs wrong side (WS)

In amigurumi there is considered to be a 'right' side (1) and a 'wrong' side (2). If you are crocheting on the right side, then your hook will be closest to you with the other edge of your crocheted piece on the other side. The tail end should be inside the piece. When starting a piece, the work naturally wants to be inside out, so just flip it the other way. Small pieces like the arms and ears need a little encouragement! Use the end of your crochet hook to turn it the other way.

Counting stitches

Keeping count of your stitches is crucial. At the end of each round there is a number in brackets which tells you how many stitches you should have at the end of that round. You'll notice when you look at the top edge of you work, there are lot of little 'v's stacked horizontally (3). Each 'v' is one stitch. Count each 'v' to determine how many stitches you have in that round.

Note: Unless otherwise stated, chains do not count as a stitch.

Tension

Tension is not critical for amigurumi, but you do need to crochet fairly tightly to keep the stitches small and minimize gaps between them (so that the stuffing doesn't show through).

If you are finding you do have gaps in your work, dropping down a hook size can help. Using an invisible decrease can also minimise gaps (see page 14). All the dolls in the book use an invisible decrease (dc2tog) rather than a regular decrease, but you can use a regular decrease if you want to.

Black and dark yarn

When working with dark yarn, especially black, make sure you have a good light source to enable you to see and count your stitches clearly.

Positioning the eyes

The position of the eyes is important: depending on where they are placed, they can give the doll different looks (4, 5 & 6). The patterns will tell you which row to place the eyes.

Changing colour

When the pattern states to change colour, do it in the last stitch of the round before, unless otherwise stated. Start a double crochet as normal (7), but for the last part of the stitch (yarn over and draw through two loops), yarn over with the new colour ready to start the next round (8). For a less visible colour change, the first stitch in the new colour should be a slip stitch (see page 13), in place of the first double crochet. Cut off the yarn of the previous colour and tie the two ends together to secure. Ends will be hidden inside the piece so there is no need to weave them in.

Stuffing the dolls

Stuff the arms and legs when you have finished making them, using small pieces of stuffing at a time. A small wooden dowel or chopstick will help you to get the stuffing in. I have a set of wooden crochet hooks that work really well (using the wrong end).

When you are crocheting the body and head, stuff as you go, again with small pieces at a time. You will be surprised how much stuffing you will need. Stuff the doll well but make sure not to over stuff, which will result in the stitches being stretched. Pay particular attention to stuffing the neck to ensure you don't get a floppy head.

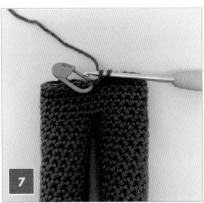

Stitches

On the following pages you will find instructions on all the stitches you'll need to use to make the dolls. If you're new to crochet, make sure you spend some time practising these with some spare yarn before you begin to make the dolls.

Slip knot

Make a loop in the yarn (1A) and then pull through a loop of yarn, place your hook onto the pulled-though loop and tighten (but don't pull tight) around your hook (1B).

Chain stitch (ch)

Make a slip knot, yarn over and pull through loop (2A). Make as many chains as the pattern states (2B). Don't pull the chain stitches too tight.

Double crochet (dc)

This is the stitch you will be using the most to create these dolls. It's a short stitch that creates a dense fabric so that stuffing does not show through. Insert hook into the next stitch (3A), yarn over and pull through, yarn over and pull through both loops (3B).

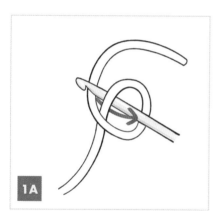

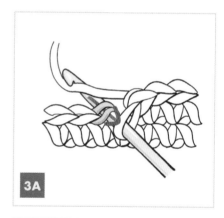

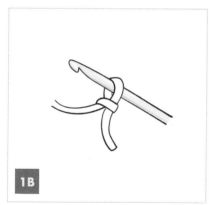

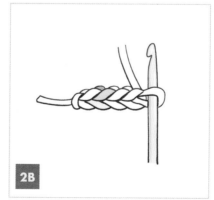

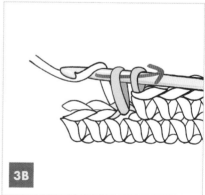

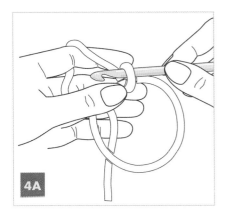

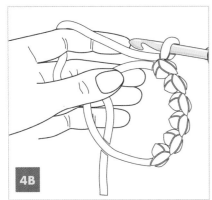

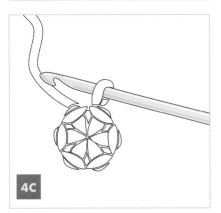

Magic ring

Also called 'magic loop' or 'magic circle'. It is used at the start of most pieces to pull the initial stitches of the first round together tightly so there is no hole. It is a very useful technique and well worth practising, even though it can seem quite daunting at first.

Wrap the yarn around your fingers and cross it over at the top, insert your hook and catch the yarn and pull through (4A), chain 1. You then make the first round of stitches into the loop (4B), which is usually six double crochet. When complete, hold the stitches in place with one hand and pull the tail end gently with the other to close the hole (4C). Pull tight to secure.

Slip stitch (sl st)

Insert hook into the next stitch, yarn over and pull through, pull through remaining loop on hook (5).

Half treble (htr)

Yarn over and insert hook into the next stitch, yarn over and pull through, yarn over and pull through all three loops (6).

Treble (tr)

Yarn over and insert hook into the next stitch, yarn over and pull through, yarn over and pull through two loops (7A), yarn over and pull through remaining two loops (7B).

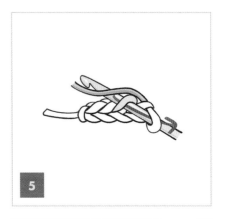

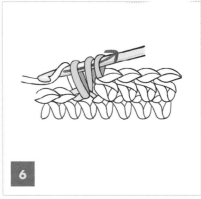

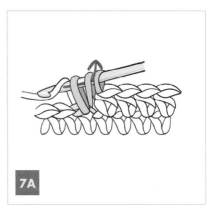

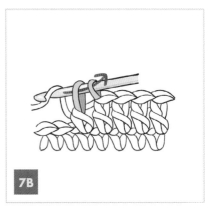

Double treble (dtr)

Yarn over 2 times and insert hook into the next stitch (8A), yarn over and pull through, yarn over and pull through 2 loops (8B), yarn over and pull through another 2 loops, yarn over and pull through remaining 2 loops (8C).

Decreasing and increasing

Decreasing and increasing stitches are important to make the shapes in amigurumi, where you will either be adding or reducing the number of stitches in a round.

When increasing, the pattern will usually say '2 dc in next st' which means you will make two double crochets in the same stitch.

When decreasing the pattern will say 'dc2tog' which means crochet two double crochet stitches together to make one. When working in rounds, the invisible decrease is used to give a neater look to the stitches. Use a regular decrease when working in rows.

INVISIBLE DECREASE
Insert hook into the front loop only (FLO) of the next stitch, do not yarn over, insert hook into FLO of next stitch (9A), yarn over and draw through two loops on hook (9B), yarn over and draw through the remaining two loops (9C).

REGULAR DECREASE
Insert hook into the next stitch, yarn over and pull through (10A), insert hook into the next stitch, yarn over and pull through, yarn over and pull through all three loops on hook (10B).

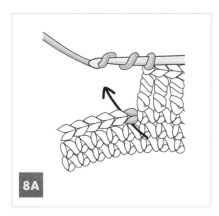

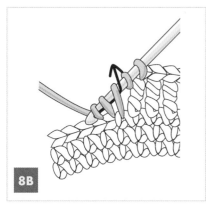

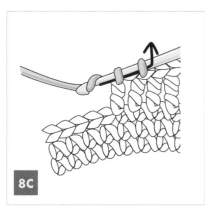

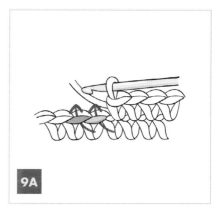

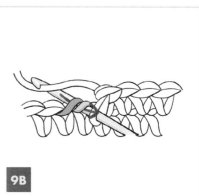

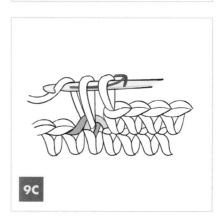

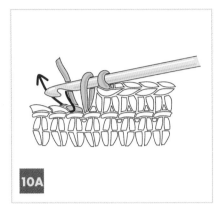

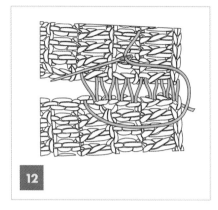

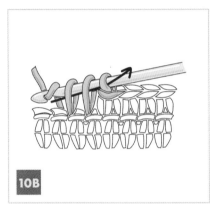

Crocheting into the back loops only (BLO)

Unless it states otherwise, you would normally make your stitches by inserting your hook into both loops of each stitch. Sometimes the pattern will tell you to insert your hook into the back loop only (BLO), in which case you insert your hook into the furthest loop from you only. This will create a row of visible front loops (11), which are then used to crochet into when joining things such as the cuffs, collar or the bottom of a coat (as for the Scientist on page 47, for example).

Mattress stitch (sewing)

Some of the accessories (such as the hi-vis jacket for the Builder on pages 38–40) will require sewing some panels together. The best sewing stitch for this is the mattress stitch.

Thread one of the tail ends onto an embroidery needle. Lay your pieces side by side and insert your needle through the bottom corner of the other piece. Take your needle back over to the other side and pass it from back to front, repeat on the other side to the end (12). You will be sewing through the rough edge of the piece and therefore there are no obvious stitches, just pass it round the stitch posts.

Body shapes

In the following pages you will find the patterns for three body shapes: A, B and C, as pictured below. Each pattern directs you to the pictures on the facing page. When you've decided on the doll you want to make, choose one of the body shapes, then follow the instructions, referring back to these pages as necessary.

9¹/₂in
(24cm)

All heights are approximate and will vary due to yarn used and tension.

8¹/₄in
(21cm)

7¹/₂in
(19cm)

A

B

C

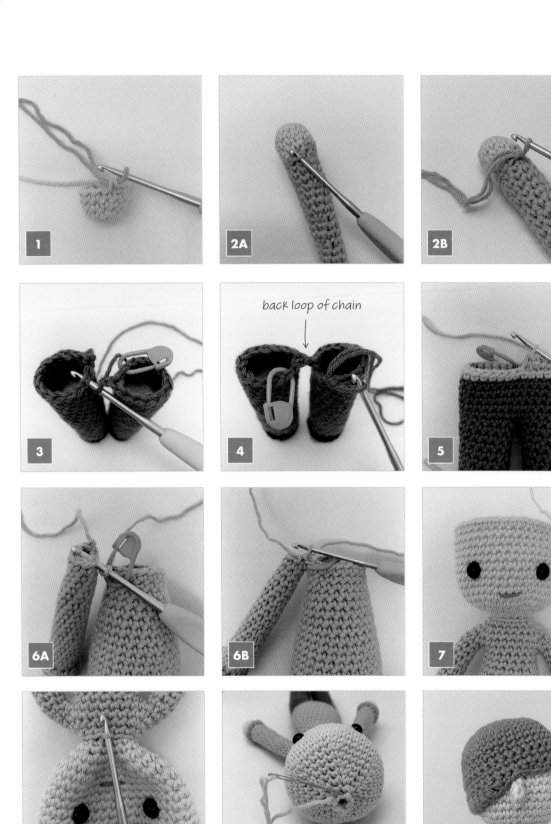

back loop of chain

Body shape A

This is the tallest of the body shapes.

ARMS
Make 2

Round 1: Using Skin colour, work into a magic ring, 6 dc. (6 sts)

Round 2: 2 dc in each st around. (12 sts)

Rounds 3–5: Dc in each st around, change to Shirt colour on last yo of last rnd. (See image 1.) (12 sts)

Round 6: Dc in each st around. (12 sts)

Round 7: In BLO dc in each st around. (12 sts)

Round 8: Dc2tog, 10 dc. (11 sts)

Rounds 9–10: Dc in each st around. (11 sts)

Round 11: Dc2tog, 9 dc. (10 sts)

Rounds 12–14: Dc in each st around. (10 sts)

Round 15: Dc2tog, 8 dc. (9 sts)

Rounds 16–17: Dc in each st around. (9 sts)

Round 18: Dc2tog, 7 dc. (8 sts)

Rounds 19–21: Dc in each st around. (8 sts)

Round 22: Dc2tog, 6 dc. (7 sts)

Rounds 23–24: Dc in each st around. (7 sts)

Round 25: 3 dc, sl st, leave the remaining sts unworked.

Fasten off leaving a long tail for sewing. Pm in next st.

CUFFS

To make the cuffs, hold arm upside down and, leaving a long starting tail, join Shirt colour to one of the FL left in round 6 (2 dc in same st, 1 dc in next st) repeat to end, sl st, fasten off and weave in ends. (See images 2A and 2B.)

LEGS
Make 2

Round 1: Using Shoe colour, work into a magic ring, 7 dc. (7 sts)

Round 2: 2 dc in each st around. (14 sts)

Rounds 3–5: Dc in each st around. (14 sts) Change to Trouser colour.

Rounds 6–25: Dc in each st around. (14 sts)

Round 26: 4 dc, sl st, leave remaining sts unworked.

Fasten off first leg, pm in next st. Do not fasten off second leg. Stuffs legs.

BODY & HEAD

Round 1: Continue with second leg, 14 dc, ch1 (counts as 1 st), starting in marked st on first leg, 14 dc, 1 dc in BLO of ch. (See images 3 and 4.) (30 sts)

Rounds 2–6: Dc in each st around. Change to Shirt colour on last yo of last rnd. (30 sts) Stuff body as you go.

Round 7: Dc in each st around (30 sts).

Round 8: In BLO dc in each st around. (See image 5.) (30 sts)

Body shape A is used for the Astronaut (page 30); Builder (page 36); Footballer (page 42); Pilot (page 70); Chef (page 100); Diver (page 106); Police officer (page 120); and Racing driver (page 126).

Rounds 9–10: Dc in each st around (30 sts). 7 dc, pm in next st to denote new start of round.
Round 11: (Dc2tog, 13 dc) twice. (28 sts)
Round 12: Dc in each st around. (28 sts)
Round 13: (Dc2tog, 12 dc) twice. (26 sts)
Round 14: Dc in each st around. (26 sts)
Round 15: (Dc2tog, 11 dc), twice. (24 sts)
Round 16: Dc in each st around (24 sts)
Round 17: (Dc2tog, 10 dc), twice. (22 sts)
Round 18: Dc in each st around. (22 sts)
Round 19: (Dc2tog, 9 dc), twice. (20 sts)
Round 20: Dc in each st around. (20 sts)
Round 21: (Dc2tog, 8 dc), twice. (18 sts)
Round 22: Dc in each st around. (18 sts)
In the next round you will join the arms, make sure to continue to mark the start of each round.
Round 23: 1 dc in next st of body, starting in marked st on first arm, 7 dc, starting in next st on body, 9 dc, starting in marked st on second arm, 7 dc, starting in next st on body 8 dc. (See images 6A and 6B.) (32 sts)
Round 24: 2 dc, dc2tog, 1 dc, dc2tog, 11 dc, dc2tog, 1 dc, dc2tog, 9 dc. (28 sts)
Round 25: (1 dc, dc2tog) twice, 9 dc, dc2tog, 1 dc, dc2tog, 8 dc. (24 sts)
Use a tapestry needle and the tail ends left on the arms to sew closed the small holes created when joining them.

Round 26: (Dc2tog, 1 dc, dc2tog, 7 dc) twice. (20 sts)
Round 27: (Dc2tog, 1 dc, dc2tog, 5 dc) twice, change to Skin colour on last yo. (16 sts)
Round 28: In BLO dc in each st around in. (16 sts)
Round 29: Dc in each st around. (16 sts)
Round 30: (2 dc in next st) 14 times, 2 dc. (30 sts)
Round 31: (2 dc in next st, 4 dc) 6 times. (36 sts)
Round 32: (2 dc in next st, 5 dc) 6 times. (42 sts)
Rounds 33–42: Dc in each st around. Secure work to continue later.
Insert safety eyes between rounds 36 and 37 and about 1 in (2.5cm) (or 8 sts) apart. Thread a tapestry needle with a short length of 010 Smoky Rose and embroider a small (½ in/1cm long) stitch for the mouth 3 rounds below the eyes. (See image 7.)

COLLAR
Row 1: Hold doll upside down and leaving a long starting tail, join Shirt colour to the FL of the front centre st of Round 27 (see image 8), ch1, 1 dc in same st as join, 16 dc (last st will be in the same st you started in), turn. (17 sts)
Row 2: Ch1, dc in each st across.
Fasten off and weave in ends.

HEAD
Continue from where you secured work, stuff as you go.
Round 43: (Dc2tog, 5 dc) 6 times. (36 sts)
Round 44: (Dc2tog, 4 dc) 6 times. (30 sts)
Round 45: (Dc2tog, 3 dc) 6 times. (24 sts)
Round 46: (Dc2tog, 2 dc) 6 times. (18 sts)
Round 47: (Dc2tog, 1 dc) 6 times. (12 sts)
Round 48: (Dc2tog) 6 times. (6 sts)
Fasten off. Thread a tapestry needle with the tail end and make some sts to pull the hole closed. (See image 9.) Weave in end.

HAIR
Make hair of your choice, see pages 24–29. Please note, if the doll you are making wears a hat, not all hairstyles will be suitable.

EARS
Make 2
Round 1: With Skin colour, work into a magic ring, 6 dc. (6 sts)
Round 2: Dc in each st around.
Sl st in next st, fasten off, leaving a long tail for sewing on.
Place the hair in position and you should see two indents where the ears should be sewn on. The ears should line up with the top of the eye, and in line with the shoulder. (See image 10.)

Body shape B

This is a medium-height body shape.

ARMS
Make 2

Round 1: Using Skin colour, work into a magic ring, 6 dc. (6 sts)

Round 2: 2 dc in each st around. (12 sts)

Rounds 3–5: Dc in each st around, change to Shirt colour on last yo of last rnd. (See image 1.) (12 sts)

Round 6: Dc in each st around. (12 sts)

Round 7: In BLO dc in each st around. (12 sts)

Round 8: Dc2tog, 10 dc. (11 sts)

Rounds 9–10: Dc in each st around. (11 sts)

Round 11: Dc2tog, 9 dc. (10 sts)

Rounds 12–13: Dc in each st around. (10 sts)

Round 14: Dc2tog, 8 dc. (9 sts)

Rounds 15–16: Dc in each st around. (9 sts)

Round 17: Dc2tog, 7 dc. (8 sts)

Rounds 18–19: Dc in each st around. (8 sts)

Round 20: Dc2tog, 6 dc. (7 sts)

Round 21: Dc in each st around. (7 sts)

Round 22: 3 dc, sl st, leave the remaining sts unworked.

Fasten off leaving a long tail for sewing. Pm in next st.

CUFFS

To make the cuffs, hold arm upside down and, leaving a long starting tail, join Shirt colour to one of the FL left in round 6 (2 dc in same st, 1 dc in next st) repeat to end, sl st, fasten off and weave in ends. (See images 2A and 2B.)

LEGS
Make 2

Round 1: Using Shoe colour, work into a magic ring, 6 dc. (6 sts)

Round 2: 2 dc in each st around. (12 sts)

Rounds 3–5: Dc in each st around. (12 sts) Change to Trouser colour.

Round 6: 2 dc in next st, 11 dc. (13 sts)

Rounds 7–9: Dc in each st around. (13 sts)

Round 10: 2 dc in next st, 12 dc. (14 sts)

Rounds 11–13: Dc in each st around. (14 sts)

Round 14: 2 dc in next st, 13 dc. (15 sts)

Rounds 15–17: Dc in each st around. (15 sts)

Round 18: 2 dc in next st, 14 dc. (16 sts)

Rounds 19–21: Dc in each st around. (16 sts)

Round 22: 6 dc, sl st, leave remaining sts unworked.

Fasten off first leg, pm in next st. Do not fasten off second leg. Stuff legs.

Body shape B is used for the Singer (page 50); Soldier (page 54); Teacher (page 60); Lumberjack (page 64); Doctor (page 86); and Firefighter (page 116).

BODY & HEAD

Round 1: Continue with second leg, 16 dc, ch1 (counts as 1 st), starting in marked st on first leg, 16 dc, 1 dc in BLO of ch. (See images 3 and 4). (34 sts)

Rounds 2–6: Dc in each st around. Change to Shirt colour on last yo of last rnd. (34 sts). Stuff body as you go.

Round 7: Dc in each st around. (34 sts).

Round 8: In BLO dc in each st around. (See image 5.) (34 sts)

Rounds 9–12: Dc in each st around. (34 sts) 9 dc, pm in next st to denote start of new round.

Round 13: (Dc2tog, 15 dc) twice. (32 sts)
Round 14: (Dc2tog, 14 dc) twice. (30 sts)
Round 15: (Dc2tog, 13 dc) twice. (28 sts)
Round 16: (Dc2tog, 12 dc) twice. (26 sts)
Round 17: (Dc2tog, 11 dc) twice. (24 sts)
Round 18: (Dc2tog, 10 dc), twice. (22 sts)
Round 19: (Dc2tog, 9 dc), twice. (20 sts)

In the next round you will join the arms, make sure to continue to mark the start of each round.

Round 20: Starting in marked st on first arm, 7 dc, starting in next st on body, 10 dc, starting in marked st on second arm, 7 dc, starting in next st on body 10 dc. (See images 6A and 6B.) (34 sts)

Round 21: (1 dc, dc2tog) twice, 12 dc, dc2tog, 1 dc, dc2tog, 11 dc. (30 sts)

Round 22: (Dc2tog, 1 dc, dc2tog, 10 dc) twice. (26 sts)

Use a tapestry needle and the tail ends left on the arms to sew closed the small holes created when joining them.

Round 23: (Dc2tog, 1 dc, dc2tog, 8 dc) twice. (22 sts)

Round 24: (Dc2tog, 1 dc, dc2tog, 6 dc) twice, change to Skin colour on last yo. (18 sts)

Round 25: In BLO, dc in each st around in. (18 sts)

Round 26: Dc in each st around. (18 sts)

Round 27: (2 dc in next st) 12 times, 6 dc. (30 sts)

Round 28: (2 dc in next st, 4 dc) 6 times. (36 sts)

Round 29: (2 dc in next st, 5 dc) 6 times. (42 sts)

Rounds 30–39: Dc in each st around. Secure work to continue later.

Insert safety eyes between rounds 32 and 33 and about (1in) 2.5cm (or 8 sts) apart. Thread a tapestry needle with a short length of 010 Smoky Rose and embroider a small (½in / 1cm long) stitch for the mouth 3 rounds below the eyes. (See image 7.)

COLLAR

Row 1: Hold doll upside down and leaving a long starting tail, join Shirt colour to the FL of the front centre st of round 24 (see image 8), ch1, 1 dc in same st as join, 18 dc (last st will be in the same st you started in), turn. (19 sts)

Row 2: Ch1, dc in each st across. Fasten off and weave in ends.

HEAD

Continue from where you secured work, stuff as you go.

Round 40: (Dc2tog, 5 dc) 6 times. (36 sts)
Round 41: (Dc2tog, 4 dc) 6 times. (30 sts)
Round 42: (Dc2tog, 3 dc) 6 times. (24 sts)
Round 43: (Dc2tog, 2 dc) 6 times. (18 sts)
Round 44: (Dc2tog, 1 dc) 6 times. (12 sts)
Round 45: (Dc2tog) 6 times. (6 sts)

Fasten off. Thread a tapestry needle with the tail end and make some sts to pull the hole closed. (See image 9.) Weave in end.

HAIR

Make hair of your choice, see pages 24–29. Please note, if the doll you are making wears a hat, not all hairstyles will be suitable.

EARS
Make 2

Round 1: With Skin colour, work into a magic ring, 6 dc. (6 sts)

Round 2: Dc in each st around.

Sl st in next st, fasten off, leaving a long tail for sewing on.

Place the hair in position and you should see two indents where the ears should be sewn on. The ears should line up with the top of the eye, and in line with the shoulder. (See image 10.)

Body shape C

This is the shortest body type.

ARMS

Make 2

Round 1: Using Skin colour, work into a magic ring, 5 dc. (5 sts)

Round 2: 2 dc in each st around. (10 sts)

Rounds 3–5: Dc in each st around, change to Shirt colour on last yo of last rnd. (See image 1.) (10 sts)

Round 6: Dc in each st around. (10 sts)

Round 7: In BLO dc in each st around. (10 sts)

Round 8: Dc2tog, 8 dc. (9 sts)

Rounds 9–11: Dc in each st around. (9 sts)

Round 12: Dc2tog, 7 dc. (8 sts)

Rounds 13–15: Dc in each st around. (8 sts)

Round 16: Dc2tog, 6 dc. (7 sts)

Rounds 17–18: Dc in each st around. (7 sts)

Round 19: 2 dc, sl st, leave the remaining sts unworked.

Fasten off leaving a long tail for sewing. Pm in next st.

CUFFS

To make the cuffs, hold arm upside down and, leaving a long starting tail, join Shirt colour to one of the FL left in round 6 (2 dc in same st, 1 dc in next st) repeat to end, sl st, fasten off and weave in ends. (See images 2A and 2B.)

LEGS

Make 2

Round 1: Using Shoe colour, work into a magic ring, 6 dc. (6 sts)

Round 2: 2 dc in each st around. (12 sts)

Rounds 3–5: Dc in each st around. (12 sts) Change to Trouser colour.

Rounds 6–18: Dc in each st around. (12 sts)

Round 19: 3 dc, sl st, leave remaining sts unworked.

Fasten off first leg, pm in next st. Do not fasten off second leg. Stuffs legs.

BODY & HEAD

Round 1: Continue with second leg, 12 dc, ch1 (counts as 1 st), starting in marked st on first leg, 12 dc, 1 dc in BLO of ch. (See images 3 and 4.) (26 sts)

Rounds 2–6: Dc around.

6 dc, pm in next st to denote start of new round. Change to Shirt colour.

Round 7: Dc in each st around.

Round 8: In BLO (dc2tog, 11 dc) twice. (See image 5.) (24 sts)

Round 9: Dc in each st around. (24 sts)

Round 10: (Dc2tog, 10 dc) twice. (22 sts)

Round 11: Dc in each st around. (22 sts)

Round 12: (Dc2tog, 9 dc) twice. (20 sts)

Round 13: Dc in each st around. (20 sts)

Round 14: (Dc2tog, 8 dc), twice. (18 sts)

Round 15: Dc in each st around. (18 sts)

In the next round you will join the arms, make sure to continue to mark the start of each round.

Body shape C is used for the Scientist (page 46); Vet (page 74); Dancer (page 82); Farmer (page 92); Athlete (page 96); and Explorer (page 110).

Round 16: 1 dc in next st of body, starting in marked st on first arm, 7 dc, starting in next st on body, 9 dc, starting in marked st on second arm, 7 dc, starting in next st on body 8 dc. (See images 6A and 6B.) (32 sts)

Round 17: 2 dc, dc2tog, 1 dc, dc2tog, 11 dc, dc2tog, 1 dc, dc2tog, 9 dc. (28 sts)

Round 18: (1 dc, dc2tog) twice, 9 dc, dc2tog, 1 dc, dc2tog, 8 dc. (24 sts)

Use a tapestry needle and the tail ends left on the arms to sew closed the small holes created when joining them.

Round 19: (Dc2tog, 1 dc, dc2tog, 7 dc) twice. (20 sts)

Round 20: (Dc2tog, 1 dc, dc2tog, 5 dc) twice, change to Skin colour on last yo. (16 sts)

Round 21: In BLO dc in each st around.

Round 22: Dc in each st around.

Round 23: (2 dc in next st) 14 times, 2 dc. (30 sts)

Round 24: (2 dc in next st, 4 dc) 6 times. (36 sts)

Round 25: (2 dc in next st, 5 dc) 6 times. (42 sts)

Rounds 26–35: Dc in each st around. Secure work to continue later.

Insert safety eyes between rounds 29 and 30 and about 1in (2.5cm), or 8 sts, apart. Thread a tapestry needle with a short length of 010 Smoky Rose and embroider a small (½in/1cm long) stitch for the mouth 3 rounds below the eyes. (See image 7.)

COLLAR

Row 1: Hold doll upside down and, leaving a long starting tail, join Shirt colour to the FL of the front centre st of Round 20 (see image 8), ch1, 1 dc in same st as join, 16 dc (last st will be in the same st you started in), turn. (17 sts)

Row 2: Ch1, dc in each st across.

Fasten off and weave in ends.

HEAD

Continue from where you secured work, stuff as you go.

Round 36: (Dc2tog, 5 dc) 6 times. (36 sts)

Round 37: (Dc2tog, 4 dc) 6 times. (30 sts)

Round 38: (Dc2tog, 3 dc) 6 times. (24 sts)

Round 39: (Dc2tog, 2 dc) 6 times. (18 sts)

Round 40: (Dc2tog, 1 dc) 6 times. (12 sts)

Round 41: (Dc2tog) 6 times. (6 sts)

Fasten off. Thread a tapestry needle with the tail end and make some sts to pull the hole closed. (See image 9.) Weave in end.

HAIR

Make hair of your choice, see pages 24–29. Please note, if the doll you are making wears a hat, not all hairstyles will be suitable.

EARS

Make 2

Round 1: With Skin colour, work into a magic ring, 6 dc. (6 sts)

Round 2: Dc in each st around.

Sl st in next st, fasten off, leaving a long tail for sewing on.

Place the hair in position and you should see two indents where the ears should be sewn on. The ears should line up with the top of the eye, and in line with the shoulder. (See image 10.)

Hairstyles

Choosing the right hairstyle for your doll is important: it adds character and brings them to life. There are ten hairstyles here and two beard options. Once you've got the hang of some of these techniques you can adapt them to create your own styles.

The hair cap is made first and then used on its own, or added to, to create different hairstyles. In most cases, the hair cap will be in the same colour as the yarn attached to create the styles. The hair cap is then sewn in place with large running stitches or can be left removable for dolls to change hairstyles. The hair is made the same size as the head to create a snug fit.

Some hairstyles are quick and simple to make, such as the hair cap and the ponytail, while others, such as the short curly hair, short hair and long hair, require more time and yarn. The main hairstyles are shown on the following pages, but some dolls include slight variations.

Note: Some hairstyles negate the need to make ears for the doll, as they will be covered up.

Hair cap

The hair cap can be used on its own as a simple hairstyle. It is also used as a base for most of the other hairstyles.

Round 1: Using Hair colour of your choice, work into a magic ring, 6 dc. (6 sts)

Round 2: 2 dc in each st around. (12 sts)

Round 3: (2 dc in next st, 1 dc) 6 times. (18 sts)

Round 4: (2 dc in next st, 2 dc) 6 times. (24 sts)

Round 5: (2 dc in next st, 3 dc) 6 times. (30 sts)

Round 6: (2 dc in next st, 4 dc) 6 times. (36 sts)

Round 7: (2 dc in next st, 5 dc) 6 times. (42 sts)

Rounds 8–11: Dc in each st around.

We will now continue in rows without a ch 1 at the start of the rows.

Row 12: Turn, skip first st, 41 dc. (41 sts)

Row 13: Turn, skip first st, 40 dc. (40 sts)

Row 14: Turn, skip first st, 39 dc. (39 sts)

Row 15: Turn, skip first st, 5 dc, 2 sl st, 1 dc, 1 htr, 15 tr, 1 htr, 1 dc, 2 sl st, 9 dc, sl st into last st. (38 sts)

Fasten off, leaving a long tail for sewing on. Place the hair onto the head. There should be a little 'dip' on each side, these line up with the ears.

HOW TO ATTACH HAIR STRANDS TO THE HAIR CAP

Refer to hair pattern on how many strands and what length each strand is required. Use a small book, plastic container or piece of card to wrap the yarn around multiple times. Then slide a small pair of scissors under the pieces of yarn to cut them all an equal length (1). Fold a strand in half. Use a 2mm hook or smaller and pass it under one of the stitch posts on the hair cap (2). Pull through the strand, then pass the ends through the loop and pull tight to secure (3).

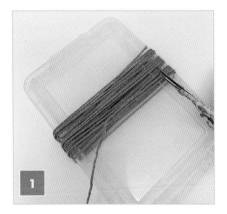

Short hair

Make hair cap in your choice of colour. In the same colour, cut around 400 strands roughly 4–4¾in (10–12cm) in length. You will need the strands fairly long to start with so you are able to attach them. They are then cut to the desired length at the end. Attach the hair strands to the hair cap. For this hairstyle you will need to attach hair under almost every stitch over the hair cap to ensure it looks full. Once all the hair has been attached trim the strands to desired length. Take your time to trim and create a nice shape.

Bob

Rounds 1–14: As hair cap in your choice of colour.

Row 15: Turn, skip first st, 37 dc, sl st. (38 sts)
Fasten off, turn and join yarn in 12th st from where you fastened off (WS).

Row 16: Ch4 (counts as one dtr), 1 dtr, 3 tr, 2 htr, 10 dc, 2 htr, 3 tr, 2 dtr. (24 sts)
Fasten off and weave in ends.

Longer bob

Rounds 1–16: As Bob.
Rounds 17–19: Turn, ch1, dc to end. (24 sts)
Fasten off and weave in ends.

Long curly hair

A good option for any doll that wears a hat.

Rounds 1–14: As hair cap in your choice of colour.

Row 15: Turn, skip first st, 37 dc, sl st. (38 sts)
Fasten off, turn and join yarn in third st in round 15 (RS).

Row 16: *Ch26, dc in 2nd chain from hook, dc in each ch to end, sl st in next st on hair cap; rep from * 23 more times.
Fasten off and weave in ends.

Bun

Make hair cap in colour of your choice.
Round 1: Using same colour, work into a magic ring, 6 dc. (6 sts)
Round 2: 2 dc in each st around. (12 sts)
Round 3: (2 dc in next st, 1 dc) 6 times. (18 sts)
Round 4: (2 dc in next st, 2 dc) 6 times. (24 sts)
Rounds 5–8: Dc in each st around. (24 sts)
Round 9: (Dc2tog, 2 dc) 6 times. (18 sts)
Round 10: (Dc2tog, 1 dc) 6 times. (12 sts)
Fasten off, leaving a long tail for sewing on. Sew the hair cap onto the head, then stuff the bun and sew in place.

Ponytail

Make hair cap in colour of your choice.
Cut around 30 strands of hair colour about 12in (30cm) long. Use a 2mm hook or smaller to add the strands around rounds 1–3 of the hair cap.

HAIR TIE

Using a 2.5mm hook ch20 in white, dc in 2nd chain from hook and dc to end. Fasten off. Wrap hair tie around the bottom of the ponytail and sew each end together. Sew to hair cap to keep in place. Weave in ends.

Plaits

Rounds 1–14: As hair cap in colour of your choice.
Row 15: Turn, skip first st, 37 dc, sl st. (38 sts) Fasten off.
Cut 30 strands of same hair colour about 10in (25cm) in length. Thread through three strands in stitches 5–9 and 25–29 of the last round of the hair cap. Do not attach by looping – pass one end all the way though making sure the ends are at the same level.
Make a plait. Decide how long you want the plait, then tie with a piece of yarn the same colour. Trim to the length required.

Short curly hair

Two to three balls of hair colour are required for this hairstyle. It's quite time consuming but worth the effort!

Round 1: Using Hair colour of your choice, work into a magic ring, 6 dc. (6 sts)

Round 2: 2 dc in each st around. (12 sts)

Round 3: In BLO (2 dc in next st, 1 dc) 6 times. (18 sts)

Round 4: (2 dc in next st, 2 dc) 6 times. (24 sts)

Round 5: In BLO (2 dc in next st, 3 dc) 6 times. (30 sts)

Round 6: (2 dc in next st, 4 dc) 6 times. (36 sts)

Round 7: In BLO (2 dc in next st, 5 dc) 6 times. (42 sts)

Rounds 8–11: Dc in each st around working into the BLO on each odd round.

We will now continue in rows without a ch 1 at the start of the rows.

Row 12: Turn, skip first st, 41 dc. (41 sts)

Row 13: Turn, skip first st, in BLO 40 dc. (40 sts)

Row 14: Turn, skip first st, 39 dc. (39 sts)

Row 15: Turn, skip first st, in BLO 38 dc. (38 sts)

Fasten off, leaving a long tail for sewing on. Join hair colour in the last BL of round 15, *ch 6, 2 dc in second ch from hook, 2 dc in each ch to end, sl st into next BL; rep from * in every BL left over the entire hair cap.

Long hair isn't suitable for dolls that wear a hat or helmet. If you are making a hat or helmet, adding hair to the lower rounds only would work (see Explorer, page 110).

Long hair

Make hair cap in your choice of colour. In the same colour cut around 150 strands roughly 10–12in (25–30cm) in length. Attach the hair strands to the hair cap. Start by attaching the strands to every other stitch in every other round. You will need to add more hair around the top of the cap and at the front where it is more visible.

Once all the hair has been attached, trim the strands to the desired length. Take your time to trim and create a nice shape.

Long hair can be styled as required – into a ponytail, bunches or left down. It can even be trimmed short for a bob (start with shorter lengths of strands for a bob).

Long beard

Cut around 60 strands about 7in (18cm) in length. The beard strands will be attached in the same way as the hair (see How to attach hair strands to the hair cap, page 25) but they are attached directly to the face and not onto a cap. Take six of the strands and attach them under the stitch posts three rounds below the eyes.

Next attach a strand just in front of the ears (or where the ears would be) and continue to add strands in a diagonal direction. Repeat for the other ear.

Add strands the next row below the initial six and two more rows beneath that. See photos below for guidance.

Short beard

Leaving long starting tail, ch7, join with sl st to first ch to create a ring.
Row 1: 6 dc into ring, turn.
Row 2: Ch5, dc in 2nd ch from hook, 2 dc, 2 dc in next st, 6 dc, turn.
Row 3: Ch5, dc in 2nd ch from hook, 2 dc, 2 dc in next st, 1 dc, 1 htr, 1 tr, 1 htr, 1 dc, sl st. Fasten off. Sew onto the face using the tail end then weave in ends.

Variations

LONG CURLY HAIR
To make the hair longer just start each curl with more chains.

For a fuller look, add curls all over the hair cap working in the BLO when making up the hair cap. (See Short Curly Hair on facing page.)

BUNCHES
Same as the ponytail but add hair at the sides of the hair instead and crochet two hair ties.

SHORT CURLY HAIR
For a less full look to Short Curly Hair, add curls to every other BL, rather than into every BL. (See Vet on page 74.) This will also use a lot less yarn.

LONG HAIR
Add hair partially to one area of the head to create another look. (See Singer on page 50.)

DOUBLE BUN
For a double bun, make two buns and sew onto the sides of the hair cap (see Dancer, below).

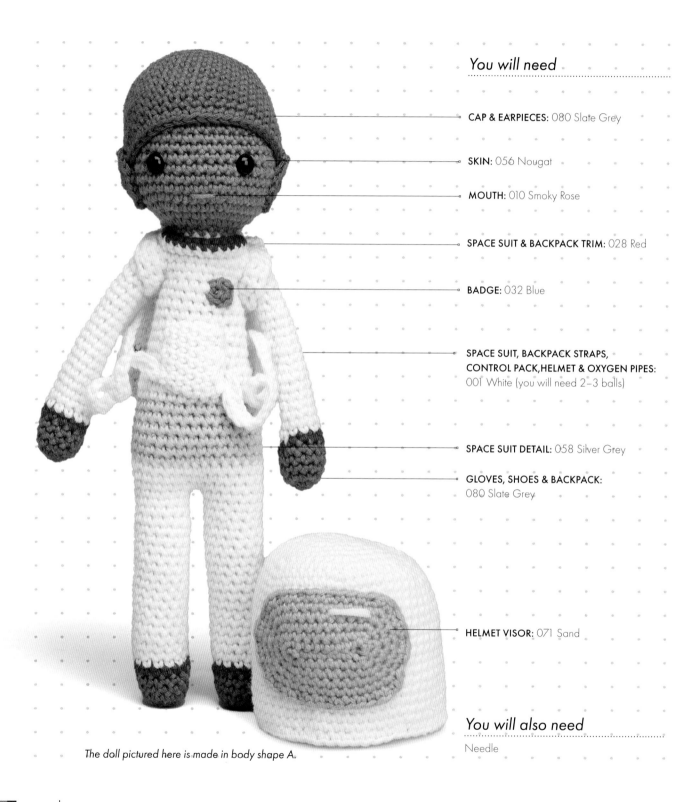

You will need

CAP & EARPIECES: 080 Slate Grey

SKIN: 056 Nougat

MOUTH: 010 Smoky Rose

SPACE SUIT & BACKPACK TRIM: 028 Red

BADGE: 032 Blue

SPACE SUIT, BACKPACK STRAPS, CONTROL PACK, HELMET & OXYGEN PIPES: 001 White (you will need 2–3 balls)

SPACE SUIT DETAIL: 058 Silver Grey

GLOVES, SHOES & BACKPACK: 080 Slate Grey

HELMET VISOR: 071 Sand

You will also need

Needle

The doll pictured here is made in body shape A.

Astronaut

Newly qualified with a Master's degree in STEM field, this astronaut will soon be arriving at the International Space Station. Orbiting the Earth approximately 240 miles (386km) above our planet, this astronaut will be conducting scientific experiments and innovative research.

Crochet each part below in order, referring to the body shape you are making (see pages 16–23).

Body shape A

ARMS
As basic pattern apart from:
Rounds 1–5: Work in Slate Grey.
Round 6: Work in Red.
Round 7: Do not work in BLO.
Rounds 8–25: Work in White.

LEGS
As basic pattern apart from:
Round 6: Work in Red.
Rounds 7–26: Work in White.

BODY & HEAD
As basic pattern apart from:
Rounds 5–10: Work in Silver Grey.
Round 8: Do not work in BLO.
Round 26: Work in BLO.
Round 28: Work in both loops.

Body shape B

ARMS
As basic pattern apart from:
Rounds 1–5: Work in Slate Grey.
Round 6: Work in Red.
Round 7: Do not work in BLO.
Rounds 8–22: Work in White.

LEGS
As basic pattern apart from:
Round 6: Work in Red.
Rounds 7–22: Work in White.

BODY & HEAD
As basic pattern apart from:
Rounds 5–10: Work in Silver Grey.
Round 8: Do not work in BLO.
Round 23: Work in BLO.
Round 25: Work in both loops.

Body shape C

ARMS
As basic pattern apart from:
Rounds 1–5: Work in Slate Grey.
Round 6: Work in Red.
Round 7: Do not work in BLO.
Rounds 8–19: Work in White.

LEGS
As basic pattern apart from:
Round 6: Work in Red.
Rounds 7–19: Work in White.

BODY & HEAD
As basic pattern apart from:
Rounds 5–10: Work in Silver Grey.
Round 8: Do not work in BLO.
Round 19: Work in BLO.
Round 21: Work in both loops.

Collar

Round 1: Join White in any FL left around neck at the back of the doll, 1 ch, 1 dc in same st, dc around.
Change to Red.
Round 2: Dc in each st around.
Sl st to close spiral.
Fasten off. Weave in ends.

Cap

Round 1: Using Slate Grey, work into a magic ring, 6 dc. (6 sts)
Round 2: 2 dc in each st to end. (12 sts)
Round 3: (2 dc in next st, 1 dc) 6 times. (18 sts)
Round 4: (2 dc in next st, 2 dc) 6 times. (24 sts)
Round 5: (2 dc in next st, 3 dc) 6 times. (30 sts)
Round 6: (2 dc in next st, 4 dc) 6 times. (36 sts)
Round 7: (2 dc in next st, 5 dc) 6 times. (42 sts)
Rounds 8–17: Dc in each st around.
Sl st to close spiral.
Fasten off leaving a long tail and sew onto the head.

Earpieces

Make 2
Round 1: Using Slate Grey, work into a magic ring, 6 dc. (6 sts)
Round 2: 2 dc in each st to end. (12 sts)
Round 3: (2 dc in next st, 1 dc) 6 times. (18 sts)
Sl st to close spiral.
Fasten off leaving a long tail for sewing onto the sides on the head, overlapping the cap.

Did you know?
An astronaut's helmet contains a small foam block so that they can scratch their noses.

Backpack

Round 1: Ch8 in Slate Grey, 2 dc in 2nd ch from hook, 5 dc, 2 dc in next st, working on the other side of the ch, 2 dc in same st, 5 dc, 2 dc in next st. (18 sts)

Round 2: 1 dc, 3 dc in next st, 6 dc, 3 dc in next st, 1 dc, 3 dc in next st, 6 dc, 3 dc in next st. (26 sts)

Round 3: 2 dc, 3 dc in next st, 8 dc, 3 dc in next st, 3 dc, 3 dc in next st, 8 dc, 3 dc in next st, 1 dc. (34 sts)

Round 4: In BLO dc in each st around.

Rounds 5–7: Dc in each st around. Change to Red. Stuff as you go.

Round 8: Dc in each st around. Change to White.

Rounds 9–22: Dc in each st around. Now, continue in rows to form the top of the bag.

1 dc (or however many required to reach the next corner of the bag).

Rows 23–27: Ch1, turn, 11 dc.

Fasten off, leaving a long tail. Use the tail to sew the top of the bag in place.

SHOULDER STRAPS
Make 2

Row 1: Ch3 in White, 1 dc in 2nd from hook, 1 dc in next ch, turn.

Rows 2–13: Ch1, 2 dc, turn.

Fasten off.

Sew one short edge to the top edge of the bag. Sew the other short edge between rounds 16–17 on the bag.

Pass each arm though a strap to place onto the back.

Badge

Make 2

Round 1: Using Blue, work into a magic ring, 6 dc. (6 sts)

Sl st to close the spiral.

Fasten off leaving a long tail for sewing on. Sew one badge onto the front of the space suit and another onto the backpack.

Front control panel

Round 1: Ch7 in White, dc in 2nd from hook, 5 dc, working on other side of the ch, dc in same st, 5 dc. (12 sts)

Rounds 2–6: Dc in each st around. (12 sts)

Fasten off and use the tail end to sew closed the open side and then to sew onto the front of the Astronaut's chest.

Oxygen pipes (optional)

Make 2

Note: Do not make if you want the backpack to be removable.

Round 1: Ch35 in White, dc in 2nd from hook and along rest of ch.

Fasten off.

Sew one end of each pipe to the front panel and sew the other end to the side of the backpack.

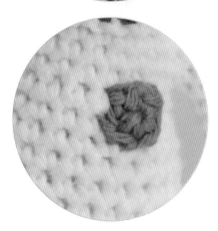

Helmet

Round 1: Using White, work into a magic ring, 6 dc. (6 sts)

Round 2: 2 dc in each st to end. (12 sts)

Round 3: (2 dc in next st, 1 dc) 6 times. (18 sts)

Round 4: (2 dc in next st, 2 dc) 6 times. (24 sts)

Round 5: (2 dc in next st, 3 dc) 6 times. (30 sts)

Round 6: (2 dc in next st, 4 dc) 6 times. (36 sts)

Round 7: (2 dc in next st, 5 dc) 6 times. (42 sts)

Round 8: (2 dc in next st, 6 dc) 6 times. (48 sts)

Rounds 9–25: Dc in each st around. (48 sts)

Round 26: (Dc2tog, 6 dc) 6 times. (42 sts) Sl st to close the spiral, fasten off and weave in end.

VISOR

Round 1: Ch9 in Sand, 2 dc in 2nd ch from hook, 6 dc, 2 dc in next st, working on other side of ch, 2 dc in same st, 6 dc, 2 dc in next st. (20 sts)

Round 2: 1 dc, 2 dc in next st, 7 dc, 2 dc in next st, 1 dc, 2 dc in next st, 7 dc, 2 dc in next st. (24 sts)

Round 3: 2 dc in next st, 1 dc, 2 dc in next st, 7 dc, 2 dc in next st, 1 dc, 2 dc in next st, 1 dc, 2 dc in next st, 7 dc, 2 dc in next st, 1 dc. (30 sts)

Round 4: (1 dc, 2 dc in next st) twice, 10 dc, (2 dc in next st, 1 dc) twice, 2 dc in next st, 10 dc, 2 dc in next st. (36 sts)

Round 5: (2 dc, 2 dc in next st) twice, 11 dc, (2 dc in next st, 2 dc) twice, 2 dc in next st, 11 dc, 2 dc in next st. (42 sts)

Round 6: 2 dc, 2 dc in next st, 3 dc, 2 dc in next st, 12 dc, (2 dc in next st, 3 dc) twice, 2 dc in next st, 12 dc, 2 dc in next st, 1 dc. (48 sts)

Sl st then fasten off.

Use White to sew a highlight onto the top right of the visor.

Sew onto front of helmet.

> The oxygen pipes and front panel add extra detail to the space suit, but it could equally be made with just the backpack. Make the helmet to complete the look.

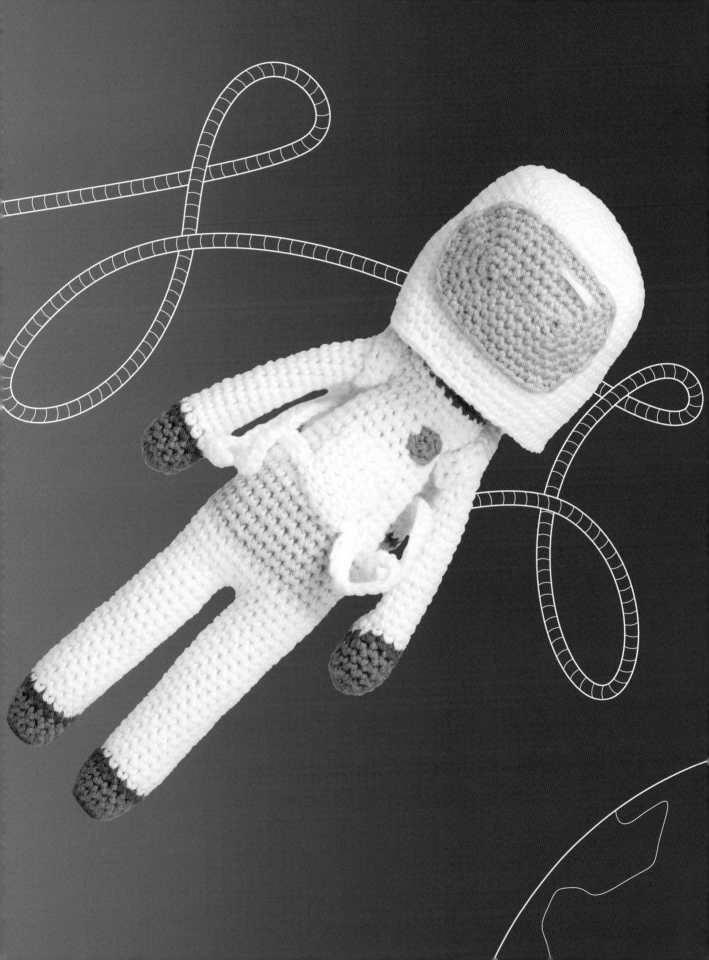

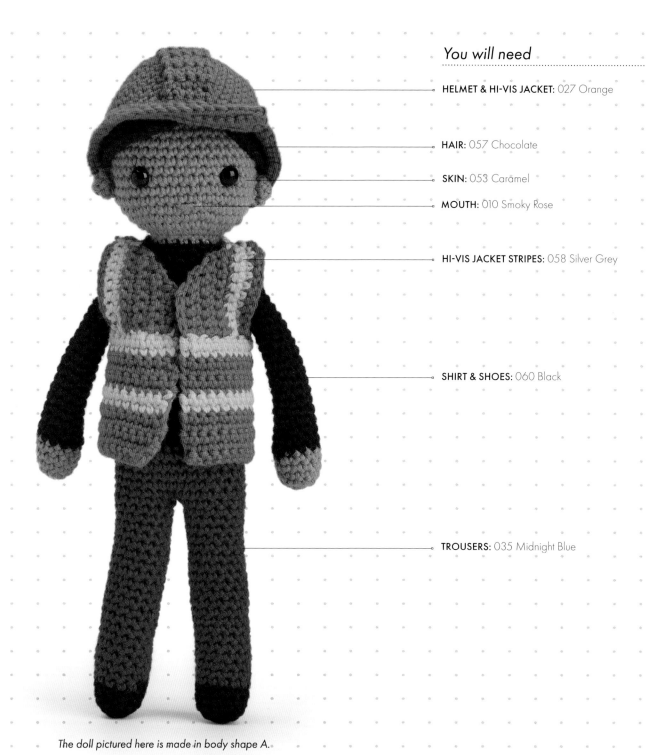

You will need

HELMET & HI-VIS JACKET: 027 Orange

HAIR: 057 Chocolate

SKIN: 053 Caramel

MOUTH: 010 Smoky Rose

HI-VIS JACKET STRIPES: 058 Silver Grey

SHIRT & SHOES: 060 Black

TROUSERS: 035 Midnight Blue

The doll pictured here is made in body shape A.

Builder

With a new set of floor plans, this builder is off to start an exciting new build. His hard hat and vest ensure his safety on site. His first job is to prepare the ground with the mini excavator ready for the foundations.

Crochet each part below in order, referring to the body shape you are making (see pages 16–23).

Body shapes A, B & C

ARMS
As basic pattern apart from:
Round 7: Work in both loops.

LEGS
As basic pattern.

BODY & HEAD
As basic pattern apart from:
Round 8: Work in both loops.

EARS
As basic pattern.

Hair

Make Hair Cap on page 24 in Chocolate.

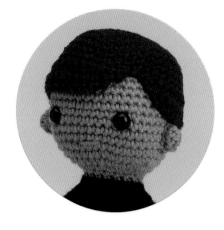

Helmet

Round 1: Using Orange, work into a magic ring, 6 dc. (6 sts)
Round 2: 2 dc in each st to end. (12 sts)
Round 3: (2 dc in next st, 1 dc) 6 times. (18 sts)
Round 4: (2 dc in next st, 2 dc) 6 times. (24 sts)
Round 5: (2 dc in next st, 3 dc) 6 times. (30 sts)
Round 6: (2 dc in next st, 4 dc) 6 times. (36 sts)
Round 7: (2 dc in next st, 5 dc) 6 times. (42 sts)
Rounds 8–14: Dc in each st around.
Round 15: (2 dc in next st, 6 dc) 6 times in FLO. (48 sts)
Round 16: 4 dc, (2 dc in next st, 7 dc) 5 times, 2 dc in next st, 3 dc. (54 sts)
Round 17: (2 dc in next st, 8 dc) 6 times. (60 sts)
Round 18: 5 dc, (2 dc in next st, 9 dc) 5 times, 2 dc in next st, 4 dc. (66 sts)
Now continue in rows to make the brim:
Row 19: Turn, skip first st, 17 dc. (17 sts)
Row 20: Turn, skip first st, 16 dc. (16 sts)
Row 21: Turn, skip first st, sl st, 13 dc, sl st. (15 sts)
Fasten off and weave in end.

HELMET RIDGE

Row 1: Ch5 in Orange.
Row 2: Dc in 2nd ch from hook, dc to end, turn. (4 sts)
Rows 3–30: Ch1, dc to end, turn.
Adjust number of rows above to fit the helmet from front to back.
Fasten off, leaving a tail for sewing.
Sew ridge in place.

Hi-vis jacket (body shape A)

The jacket is made up of four panels then sewn together using the tail ends.

LOWER PANEL
Make 1

Row 1: Ch39 in Orange, dc in 2nd ch from hook, dc to end of ch, turn. (38 sts)
Rows 2–5: Ch1, dc across, turn. (38 sts)
Change to Silver Grey.
Rows 6–7: Ch1, dc across, turn. (38 sts)
Change to Orange.
Rows 8–11: Ch1, dc across, turn. (38 sts)
Change to Silver Grey.
Rows 12–13: Ch1, dc across, turn. (38 sts)
Fasten off.

UPPER BACK PANEL
Make 1

Row 1: Ch11 in orange, dc in 2nd ch from hook, dc to end of ch, turn. (10 sts)
Row 2: Ch1, dc across, turn. (10 sts)
Change to Silver Grey.
Rows 3–4: Ch1, dc across, turn. (10 sts)
Change to Orange.
Rows 5–14: Ch1, dc across, turn. (10 sts)
Change to Silver Grey.
Rows 15–16: Ch1, dc across, turn. (10 sts)
Change to Orange.
Rows 17–18: Ch1, dc across, turn. (10 sts)
Fasten off.

UPPER FRONT PANELS
Make 2
Note: Use regular decreases here, not invisible decreases.

Row 1: Ch11 in orange, dc in 2nd ch from hook, dc to end of ch, turn. (10 sts)
Change to Silver Grey.

Rows 2–3: Ch1, dc across, turn. (10 sts)
Change to Orange.

Row 4: Ch1, dc2tog, 8 dc, turn. (9 sts)
Row 5: Ch1, 7 dc, dc2tog, turn. (8 sts)
Row 6: Ch1, dc2tog, 6 dc, turn. (7 sts)
Row 7: Ch1, 5 dc, dc2tog, turn. (6 sts)
Row 8: Ch1, dc2tog, 4 dc, turn. (5 sts)
Row 9: Ch1, 3 dc, dc2tog, turn. (4 sts)
Row 10: Ch1, dc2tog, 2 dc, turn. (3 sts)
Fasten off.

Weave in most of the ends apart from a few for sewing together. Block (see box on page 40) then sew the panels together using the diagram on page 40 as a guide and mattress stitch (see page 15).

Hi-vis jacket (body shape B)

The jacket is made up of four panels then sewn together using the tail ends.

LOWER PANEL
Make 1
Row 1: Ch43 in Orange, dc in 2nd ch from hook, dc to end of ch, turn. (42 sts)

Rows 2–4: Ch1, dc across, turn. (42 sts)
Change to Silver Grey.

Rows 5–6: Ch1, dc across, turn. (42 sts)
Change to Orange.

Rows 7–9: Ch1, dc across, turn. (42 sts)
Change to Silver Grey.

Rows 10–11: Ch1, dc across, turn. (42 sts)
Fasten off.

UPPER BACK PANEL
Make 1
Row 1: Ch11 in orange, dc in 2nd ch from hook, dc to end of ch, turn. (10 sts)
Row 2: Ch1, dc across, turn. (10 sts)
Change to Silver Grey.

Rows 3–4: Ch1, dc across, turn. (10 sts)
Change to Orange.

Rows 5–14: Ch1, dc across, turn. (10 sts)
Change to Silver Grey.

Rows 15–16: Ch1, dc across, turn. (10 sts)
Change to Orange.

Rows 17–18: Ch1, dc across, turn. (10 sts)
Fasten off.

UPPER FRONT PANELS
Make 2
Note: Use regular decreases here, not invisible decreases.

Row 1: Ch11 in orange, dc in 2nd ch from hook, dc to end of ch, turn. (10 sts)
Change to Silver Grey.

Rows 2–3: Ch1, dc across, turn. (10 sts)
Change to Orange.

Rows 4–5: Ch1, dc across, turn. (10 sts)
Row 6: Ch1, dc2tog, 8 dc, turn. (9 sts)
Row 7: Ch1, 7 dc, dc2tog, turn. (8 sts)
Row 8: Ch1, dc2tog, 6 dc, turn. (7 sts)
Row 9: Ch1, 5 dc, dc2tog, turn. (6 sts)
Row 10: Ch1, dc2tog, 4 dc, turn. (5 sts)
Row 11: Ch1, 3 dc, dc2tog, turn. (4 sts)
Row 12: Ch1, dc2tog, 2 dc, turn. (3 sts)
Fasten off.

Weave in most of the ends apart from a few for sewing together. Block (see box on page 40) then the panels together using the diagram on page 40 as a guide and mattress stitch (see page 15).

Hi-vis jacket (body shape C)

The jacket is made up of four panels then sewn together using the tail ends.

LOWER PANEL
Make 1
Row 1: Ch35 in Orange, dc in 2nd ch from hook, dc to end of ch, turn. (34 sts)
Rows 2–3: Ch1, dc across, turn. (34 sts)
Change to Silver Grey.
Rows 4–5: Ch1, dc across, turn. (34 sts)
Change to Orange.
Rows 6–7: Ch1, dc across, turn. (34 sts)
Change to Silver Grey.
Rows 8–9: Ch1, dc across, turn. (34 sts)
Fasten off.

UPPER BACK PANEL
Make 1
Row 1: Ch9 in orange, dc in 2nd ch from hook, dc to end of ch, turn. (8 sts)
Row 2: Ch1, dc across, turn. (8 sts)
Change to Silver Grey.
Rows 3–4: Ch1, dc across, turn. (8 sts)
Change to Orange.
Rows 5–13: Ch1, dc across, turn. (8 sts)
Change to Silver Grey.
Rows 14–15: Ch1, dc across, turn. (8 sts)
Change to Orange.
Rows 16–17: Ch1, dc across, turn. (8 sts)
Fasten off.

UPPER FRONT PANELS
Make 2
Note: Use regular decreases here, not invisible decreases.
Row 1: Ch9 in orange, dc in 2nd ch from hook, dc to end of ch, turn. (8 sts)
Change to Silver Grey.
Rows 2–3: Ch1, dc across, turn. (8 sts)
Change to Orange.
Row 4: Ch1, dc2tog, 6 dc, turn. (7 sts)
Row 5: Ch1, 5 dc, dc2tog, turn. (6 sts)
Row 6: Ch1, dc2tog, 4 dc, turn. (5 sts)
Row 7: Ch1, 3 dc, dc2tog, turn. (4 sts)
Row 8: Ch1, dc2tog, 2 dc, turn. (3 sts)
Fasten off.

Weave in most of the ends apart from a few for sewing together. Block (see box on right) then sew the panels together using the diagram as a guide and mattress stitch (see page 15).

Blocking
This is recommended before sewing. Use a foam blocking board or a folded towel to pin the pieces down. Spray with water then allow to dry overnight. This should stop the corners curling up so much.

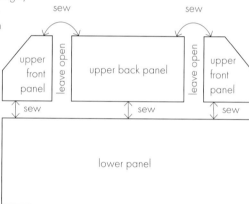

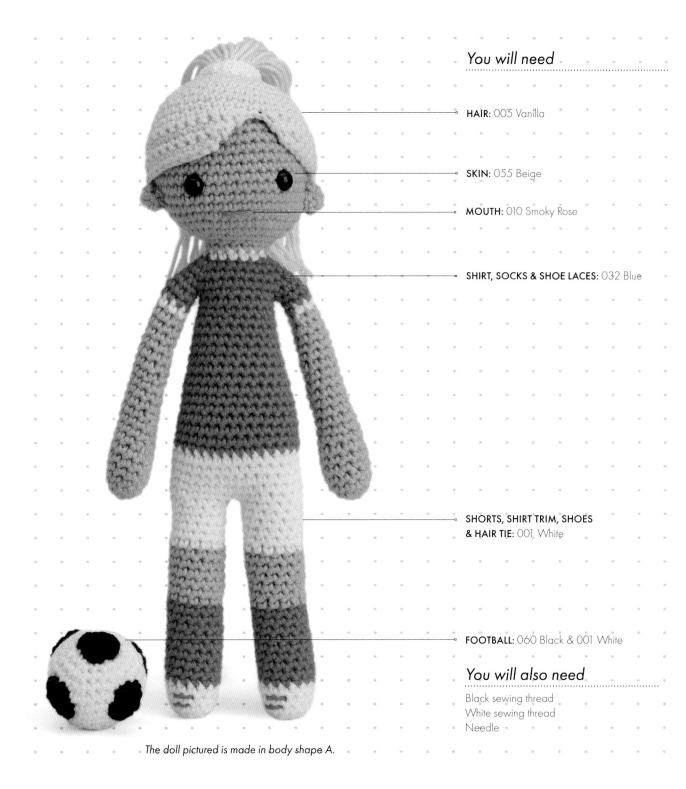

You will need

HAIR: 005 Vanilla

SKIN: 055 Beige

MOUTH: 010 Smoky Rose

SHIRT, SOCKS & SHOE LACES: 032 Blue

SHORTS, SHIRT TRIM, SHOES & HAIR TIE: 001 White

FOOTBALL: 060 Black & 001 White

You will also need

Black sewing thread
White sewing thread
Needle

The doll pictured is made in body shape A.

Footballer

This footballer is training for a big match at the weekend. Training starts at 8am every morning with a workout and stretches. Next, a healthy breakfast and then training begins on the pitch with warm-ups and passing drills.

Crochet each part below in order, referring to the body shape you are making (see pages 16–23).

Body shape A

ARMS
As basic pattern apart from:
Rounds 1–21: Work in Skin colour.
(Do not work in BLO in round 7.)
Round 22: Work in White.
Rounds 23–25: Work in Blue.

LEGS
As basic pattern apart from:
Rounds 6–14: Work in Blue.
Round 15: Work 2 dc in Blue, work remaining stitches in Skin colour.
Rounds 16–20: Work in Skin colour.
Round 21: Work 4 dc in Skin colour, work remaining stitches in White.
Rounds 21–26: Work in White.

BODY & HEAD
As basic pattern apart from:
Round 8: Do not work in BLO.
Round 27: Work in White.

Body shape B

ARMS
As basic pattern apart from:
Rounds 1–18: Work in Skin colour.
(Do not work in BLO in round 7.)
Round 19: Work in White.
Rounds 20–22: Work in Blue.

LEGS
As basic pattern apart from:
Rounds 6–12: Work in Blue.
Round 13: Work 2 dc in Blue, work remaining stitches in Skin colour.
Rounds 14–18: Work in Skin colour.
Round 19: Work 4 dc in Skin colour, work remaining stitches in White.
Rounds 20–22: Work in White.

BODY & HEAD
As basic pattern apart from:
Round 8: Do not work in BLO.
Round 24: Work in White.

Body shape C

ARMS
As basic pattern apart from:
Rounds 1–15: Work in Skin colour.
(Do not work in BLO in round 7.)
Round 16: Work in White.
Rounds 17–19: Work in Blue.

LEGS
As basic pattern apart from:
Rounds 6–11: Work in Blue.
Round 12: Work 2 dc in Blue, work remaining stitches in Skin colour.
Rounds 13–15: Work in Skin colour.
Round 16: Work 4 dc in Skin colour, work remaining stitches in White.
Rounds 17–19: Work in White.

BODY & HEAD
As basic pattern apart from:
Round 8: Do not work in BLO.
Round 20: Work in White.

Ears

As basic pattern, for all body shapes.

Hair

Make Ponytail on page 27 in Vanilla.

Shoes

Using Blue sew two small stitches on the front of each shoe for laces.

Shirt number (9)

Ch 19 in White, dc in 2nd ch from hook and along rest of chain.
Fasten off.
Sew one end to create the 9 shape, then use white sewing thread to sew onto the back of the shirt.
Other numbers can be created using this method – you will just have to adjust the length and number of pieces.

Football

Round 1: Using White, work into a magic ring, 6 dc. (6 sts)
Round 2: 2 dc in each st to end. (12 sts)
Round 3: (2 dc in next st, 1 dc) 6 times. (18 sts)
Round 4: (2 dc in next st, 2 dc) 6 times. (24 sts)
Round 5: (2 dc in next st, 3 dc) 6 times. (30 sts)
Rounds 6–10: Dc in each st around. (30 sts)
Round 11: (Dc2tog, 3 dc) 6 times. (24 sts)
Round 12: (Dc2tog, 2 dc) 6 times. (18 sts)
Round 13: (Dc2tog, 1 dc) 6 times. (12 sts)
Round 14: (Dc2tog) 6 times. (6 sts)
Fasten off.
Thread a tapestry needle with the tail end and make some sts to pull the hole closed.
Weave in end.

PENTAGONS
Make about 6
Round 1: Using Black, work into a magic ring (1 dc, 1 tr) 5 times. (10 sts)
Making sure your sts are straight, pull the magic circle gently to close, sl st to the first dc to join spiral.
Fasten off.
Weave in end.
Use black sewing thread and a needle to sew the pentagons onto the football.

Did you know?
Women's football was banned in England in 1921 for being 'quite unsuitable for females and ought not to be encouraged'. The ban was finally lifted 50 years later in 1971.

You will need

HAIR: 025 Fox

SKIN: 065 Blush

GOGGLES: 058 Silver Grey

MOUTH: 010 Smoky Rose

COAT & TEST TUBE: 001 White

TEST-TUBE POTION: 046 Light Green

TROUSERS: 059 Mouse Grey

SHOES & GOGGLE STRAPS: 060 Black

The doll pictured is made in body shape C.

Scientist

With a PhD in microbiology, this scientist is in the laboratory observing micro-organisms through her microscope. She is currently researching a particularly virulent microbe in hope of developing a new vaccine.

Crochet each part below in order, referring to the body shape you are making (see pages 16–23).

Body shapes A, B & C

ARMS
As basic pattern.

CUFFS
As basic pattern.

LEGS
As basic pattern.

BODY & HEAD
As basic pattern.

COLLAR
As basic pattern.

Bottom of coat

Row 1: Hold doll upside down and, leaving a long starting tail, join White colour to the FL of the front centre st of Round 7 of body, ch1, 1 dc in same st as join, dc in each st around, dc into the first st you started, turn.
Round 2: Ch1, dc in each st around with 2 increases, one on each side of the doll, turn.
Round 3: Ch1, dc in each st around, turn.
Round 4: Ch1, dc in each st around with 2 increases, one on each side of the doll, turn.
Round 5: Ch1, dc in each st around, turn.
Round 6: Ch1, dc in each st around with 2 increases, one on each side of the doll, turn.
Round 7: Ch1, dc in each st around.
Fasten off. Weave in ends.

Hair

Make Plaits (see page 27) in Fox.

Goggles

Ch38 in Silver Grey.
Fasten off and weave in ends.
Position the ends side by side and sew
together, then sew the ends midway along
chain (see diagrams on the right).

GOGGLE STRAP
Ch35 in Black.
Fasten off.
Sew one end to either side of the goggles.
Weave in ends.

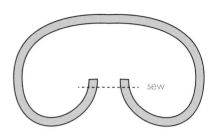

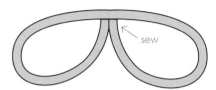

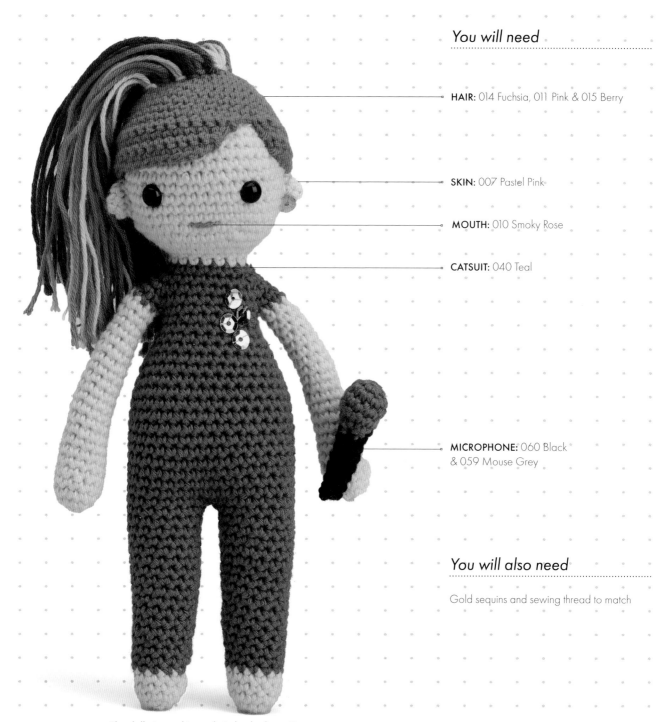

You will need

HAIR: 014 Fuchsia, 011 Pink & 015 Berry

SKIN: 007 Pastel Pink

MOUTH: 010 Smoky Rose

CATSUIT: 040 Teal

MICROPHONE: 060 Black & 059 Mouse Grey

You will also need

Gold sequins and sewing thread to match

The doll pictured is made in body shape B.

Singer

In her sparkly teal catsuit this singer is all ready for her big gig tonight. She is slightly nervous playing in front of her biggest audience yet, but she's ready for the spotlight with her band and backing singers.

Crochet each part below in order, referring to the body shape you are making (see pages 16–23).

Body shape A

ARMS
As basic pattern but work all in Skin colour.

LEGS
As basic pattern apart from:
Rounds 1–5: Work in Skin colour.

BODY & HEAD
As basic pattern apart from:
Rounds 1–27: Work all in Teal.
(Do not work in BLO in round 8.)

EARS
As basic pattern.

Body shape B

ARMS
As basic pattern but work all in Skin colour.

LEGS
As basic pattern apart from:
Rounds 1–5: Work in Skin colour.

BODY & HEAD
As basic pattern apart from:
Rounds 1–24: Work all in Teal.
(Do not work in BLO in round 8.)

EARS
As basic pattern.

Body shape C

ARMS
As basic pattern but work all in Skin colour.

LEGS
As basic pattern apart from:
Rounds 1–5: Work in Skin colour.

BODY & HEAD
As basic pattern apart from:
Rounds 1–20: Work all in Teal.
(Do not work in BLO in round 8.)

EARS
As basic pattern.

Hair

As Long Hair on page 28 apart from:
Use about 50 strands in a mix of the hair colours and attach in a small area over the first few rounds of the hair cap.

Top

Sew some sequins onto the top.

Earring

Sew a sequin onto one or both ears.

Microphone

Round 1: Using Mouse Grey, work into a magic ring, 6 dc. (6 sts)
Round 2: 2 dc in each st around. (12 sts)
Rounds 3–4: Dc in each st around. (12 sts)
Round 5: (Dc2tog) 6 times. (6 sts)
Stuff and change to Black.
Rounds 6–12: Dc in each st around.
Fasten off and use the tail end to sew the bottom closed. Weave in end.

The catsuit could be made in a range of bright colours. Crocheting the catsuit in black with the gold sequins would also look great.

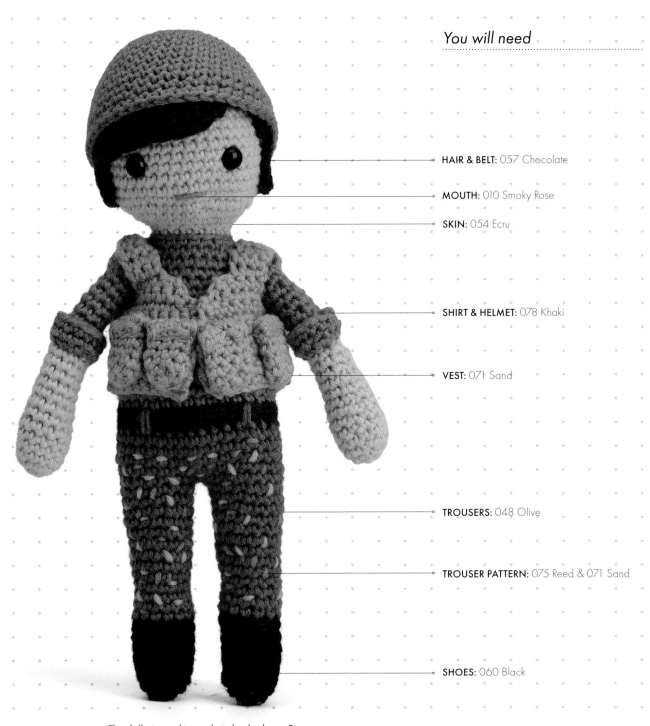

HAIR & BELT: 057 Chocolate

MOUTH: 010 Smoky Rose

SKIN: 054 Ecru

SHIRT & HELMET: 078 Khaki

VEST: 071 Sand

TROUSERS: 048 Olive

TROUSER PATTERN: 075 Reed & 071 Sand

SHOES: 060 Black

The doll pictured is made in body shape B.

Soldier

This soldier has finished her military training and is off to join her regiment. She is now embarking on a training course to become a cyber security engineer, where she will learn how to install telecommunications.

Crochet each part below in order, referring to the body shape you are making (see pages 16–23).

Body shape A

ARMS
As basic pattern apart from:
Rounds 1–18: Work in Skin colour.
(Do not work in BLO in round 7.)
Change to Khaki.
Round 19: Work in BLO.

CUFFS
Hold arm right way up and join Khaki into a FL left in round 18.
Round 1: (2 dc in next st, 3 dc) twice. (10 sts)
Round 2: (2 dc in next st, 4 dc) twice. (12 sts)
Round 3: Dc in each st to end. (12 sts)
Fasten off and weave in ends. Make sure cuff is folded back.

LEGS
As basic pattern apart from:
Rounds 1–11: Work in Black.
Change to Olive.
Do not stuff legs.

BODY & HEAD
As basic pattern apart from:
Secure work with a st marker after round 6.
Take an embroidery needle and a length of Reed and sew small sts all over the trousers.
Repeat with a length of Khaki.
Rounds 7–8: Work in Chocolate.
(Do not work in BLO in round 8.)
Round 9: Work in Khaki in BLO.

Body shape B

ARMS
As basic pattern apart from:
Rounds 1–13: Work in Skin colour.
(Do not work in BLO in round 7.)
Change to Khaki colour.
Round 14: Work in BLO.

CUFFS
Hold arm right way up and join Khaki into a FL left in round 13.
Round 1: (2 dc in next st, 4 dc) twice. (12 sts)
Round 2: (2 dc in next st, 5 dc) twice. (14 sts)
Round 3: Dc in each st to end. (14 sts)
Fasten off and weave in ends. Make sure cuff is folded back.

LEGS
As basic pattern apart from:
Rounds 1–9: Work in Black.
Change to Olive.
Do not stuff legs.

BODY & HEAD
As basic pattern apart from:
Secure work with a st marker after round 6.
Take an embroidery needle and a length of Reed and sew small sts all over the trousers.
Repeat with a length of Khaki.
Rounds 7–8: Work in Chocolate.
(Do not work in BLO in round 8.)
Round 9: Work in Khaki in BLO.

Body shape C

ARMS
As basic pattern apart from:
Rounds 1–13: Work in Skin colour.
(Do not work in BLO in round 7.)
Change to Khaki colour.
Round 14: Work in BLO.

CUFFS
Hold arm right way up and join Khaki into a FL left in round 13.
Round 1: (2 dc in next st, 3 dc) twice. (10 sts)
Round 2: (2 dc in next st, 4 dc) twice. (12 sts)
Round 3: Dc in each st to end. (12 sts)
Fasten off and weave in ends. Make sure cuff is folded back.

LEGS
As basic pattern apart from:
Rounds 1–9: Work in Black.
Change to Olive.
Do not stuff legs.

BODY & HEAD
As basic pattern apart from:
Secure work with a st marker after round 6.
Take an embroidery needle and a length of Reed and sew small sts all over the trousers.
Repeat with a length of Khaki.
Rounds 7–8: Work in Chocolate.
(Do not work in BLO in round 8.)
Round 9: Work in Khaki in BLO.

Hair

Make Bob (see page 26).

Belt loops

Use Olive to sew a couple of small stitches over round 7 to create belt loops.

Helmet

Round 1: Using Khaki, work into a magic ring, 6 dc. (6 sts)
Round 2: 2 dc in each st to end. (12 sts)
Round 3: (2 dc in next st, 1 dc) 6 times. (18 sts)
Round 4: (2 dc in next st, 2 dc) 6 times. (24 sts)
Round 5: (2 dc in next st, 3 dc) 6 times. (30 sts)
Round 6: (2 dc in next st, 4 dc) 6 times. (36 sts)
Round 7: (2 dc in next st, 5 dc) 6 times. (42 sts)
Rounds 8–15: Dc in each st around. Fasten off and weave in ends or use the tail end to sew in place.

Vest (body shape A)

Row 1: Ch39 in Sand, dc in 2nd ch from hook, dc to end of ch, turn. (38 sts)
Rows 2–11: Ch1, dc across, turn. (38 sts)
Row 12: Ch1, dc2tog, 34 dc, dc2tog. (36 sts)
Row 13: Ch1, dc2tog, 32 dc, dc2tog. (34 sts)
Row 14: Ch1, dc2tog, 3 dc, leave remaining sts unworked, turn. (4 sts)
Row 15: Ch1, 3 dc, leave remaining st unworked, turn. (3 sts)
Rows 16–19: Ch1, 3 dc, turn. (3 sts)
Fasten off. Join yarn in 4th stitch on main panel from strap just made.
Rows 1–4: Ch1, 18 dc, turn. (18 sts)
Row 5: Dc2tog, 14 dc, dc2tog. (16 sts)
Row 6: Dc2tog, 12 dc, dc2tog. (14 sts)
Fasten off. Join yarn in last st on main panel.
Row 1: Ch1, dc2tog, 3 dc, leave remaining sts unworked, turn. (4 sts)
Row 2: Ch1, 3 dc, leave remaining st unworked, turn. (3 sts)
Rows 3–6: Ch1, 3 dc, turn. (3 sts)
Fasten off.

Block (see box below) then fold the side panels in and sew the top of the straps to the top of the corners of the back panel.

Vest (body shape B)

Row 1: Ch43 in Sand, dc in 2nd ch from hook, dc to end of ch, turn. (42 sts)
Rows 2–8: Ch1, dc across, turn. (42 sts)
Row 9: Ch1, dc2tog, 38 dc, dc2tog. (40 sts)
Row 10: Ch1, dc2tog, 36 dc, dc2tog. (38 sts)
Row 11: Ch1, dc2tog, 3 dc, leave remaining sts unworked, turn. (4 sts)
Row 12: Ch1, 3 dc, leave remaining st unworked, turn. (3 sts)
Rows 13–16: Ch1, 3 dc, turn. (3 sts)
Fasten off. Join yarn in 5th stitch on main panel from strap just made.
Rows 1–4: Ch1, 20 dc, turn. (20 sts)
Row 5: Dc2tog, 16 dc, dc2tog. (18 sts)
Row 6: Dc2tog, 14 dc, dc2tog. (16 sts)
Fasten off. Join yarn in last st on main panel.
Row 1: Ch1, dc2tog, 3 dc, leave remaining sts unworked, turn. (4 sts)
Row 2: Ch1, 3 dc, leave remaining st unworked, turn. (3 sts)
Rows 3–6: Ch1, 3 dc, turn. (3 sts)
Fasten off.

Block (see box below) then fold the side panels in and sew the top of the straps to the top of the corners of the back panel.

Vest (body shape C)

Row 1: Ch35 in Sand, dc in 2nd ch from hook, dc to end of ch, turn. (34 sts)
Rows 2–8: Ch1, dc across, turn. (34 sts)
Row 9: Ch1, dc2tog, 30 dc, dc2tog. (32 sts)
Row 10: Ch1, dc2tog, 28 dc, dc2tog. (30 sts)
Row 11: Ch1, dc2tog, 3 dc, leave remaining sts unworked, turn. (4 sts)
Row 12: Ch1, 3 dc, leave remaining st unworked, turn. (3 sts)
Rows 13–15: Ch1, 3 dc, turn. (3 sts)
Fasten off. Join yarn in 3rd stitch on main panel from strap just made.
Rows 1–3: Ch1, 16 dc, turn. (16 sts)
Row 4: Dc2tog, 12 dc, dc2tog. (14 sts)
Row 5: Dc2tog, 10 dc, dc2tog. (12 sts)
Fasten off. Join yarn in last st on main panel.
Row 1: Ch1, dc2tog, 3 dc, leave remaining sts unworked, turn. (4 sts)
Row 2: Ch1, 3 dc, leave remaining st unworked, turn. (3 sts)
Rows 3–5: Ch1, 3 dc, turn. (3 sts)
Fasten off.

Block (see box below) then fold the side panels in and sew the top of the straps to the top of the corners of the back panel.

To make a complete camouflage uniform, crochet the arms as the basic pattern in the same colour as the trousers and continue the pattern detail. You could also do the same for the helmet.

Blocking
This is recommended before sewing. Use a foam blocking board or a folded towel to pin the pieces down. Spray with water then allow to dry overnight. This should stop the corners curling up so much.

POCKETS FOR VEST
Make 4
Round 1: Ch5 in Sand, dc in 2nd ch from hook, 3 dc, working in other side of ch, dc in same st, 3 dc. (8 sts)

Rounds 2–5: Dc in each st around. Now, continue in rows to form the top flap.

Row 6: Turn, ch1, 4 dc, turn. (4 sts)

Row 7: Ch1, 4 dc. (4 sts)

Fasten off and use the tail end to sew the flap down.

Sew the pockets onto the front of the vest. Place the vest on the doll and sew the front seam of the vest together to secure in place, or leave it open for it to be removable.

Did you Know?
In 2005, special antimicrobial underwear was developed that soldiers could wear for up to three months at a time without needing to be changed.

You will need

HAIR: 060 Black

SKIN: 057 Chocolate

MOUTH: 010 Smoky Rose

SHIRT: 034 Denim

SATCHEL: 035 Midnight Blue
& 058 Silver Grey

TROUSERS: 071 Sand

BOOKS: 026 Tangerine, 043 Ivy,
029 Wine Red & 002 Cream

SHOES & BELT: 056 Nougat

The doll pictured here is made in body shape B.

Teacher

There are 30 excited and nervous primary children soon to arrive in class.
This teacher is looking forward to starting a new school year with them and hopes
he can inspire them with their first topic – space!

Crochet each part below in order, referring to the body shape you are making (see pages 16–23).

Body shapes A, B & C

ARMS
As basic pattern.

CUFFS
As basic pattern.

LEGS
As basic pattern.

BODY & HEAD
As basic pattern apart from:
Round 7: Work in Nougat.
Round 8: Work in Denim in BLO.

COLLAR
As basic pattern.

Hair

Make Short Curly Hair on page 28
in Black.

Belt loops

Use Sand to sew a couple of small stitches over round 7 to create belt loops.

Braces (optional)

Make 2
Ch35 in Nougat. (Adjust length for different body shapes.)
Fasten off.
Sew one end of each brace to the top of the belt at the front. Pass the brace over the shoulder and cross over at the back and sew in place. You may need a little stitch on the shoulder to keep in place.

Books

Make as many as you want
PAGES
Row 1: Ch8 in Cream, dc in 2nd ch from hook, dc to end of ch, turn. (7 sts)
Rows 2–11: Ch1, dc across, turn. (7 sts)
Fasten off and weave in ends.

COVER
Row 1: Ch9 in Wine Red, Tangerine or Ivy, dc in 2nd ch from hook, dc to end of ch, turn. (8 sts)
Rows 2–14: Ch1, dc across, turn. (8 sts)
Fasten off. Place the pages on top of the cover and fold both in half. Use the tail end to sew through all layers to secure. Weave in any remaining ends.

Glasses (optional)

The toy glasses can be purchased online (see Suppliers, page 133). They measure 1¾ x ¾in (4.6 x 1.8cm).

Satchel

Row 1: Ch13 in Midnight Blue, dc in 2nd ch from hook, dc to end of ch, turn. (12 sts)
Rows 2–21: Ch1, dc across, turn. (12 sts)
Row 22: Dc2tog, 8 dc, dc2tog. (10 sts)
Row 23: Dc2tog, 6 dc, dc2tog. (8 sts)
Fasten off. Fold the bottom short edge up, then the top edge down to create the satchel shape. Use the tail end to sew in place.

FASTENINGS
Make 2
Row 1: Ch4 in Midnight Blue, dc in 2nd ch from hook, dc to end of ch, turn. (3 sts)
Fasten off. Sew each strap to the edge of the satchel. Sew two small stitches in Silver grey for buckles.

SHOULDER STRAP
Row 1: Ch41 in Midnight Blue, dc in 2nd ch from hook, dc to end of ch, turn. (40 sts)
Fasten off then sew to the top corners of the satchel.

Did you know?
A pupil will spend on average a minimum of 15,960 hours at school (which is just under 2 years).

DEERSTALKER BRIM: 052 Light Brown

SKIN: 055 Beige

HAIR & BEARD: 057 Chocolate

SHIRT & DEERSTALKER HAT:
060 Black & 029 Wine Red

BRACES: 028 Red

TROUSERS: 034 Denim

SHOES, BELT & CUFFS: 060 Black

The doll pictured here is made in body shape B.

Lumberjack

Despite being one of the most dangerous jobs, this lumberjack (or logger) loves working every day in the great outdoors among the trees; an office job is not for him. Today he will be using the skidder to transport already felled trees.

Crochet each part below in order, referring to the body shape you are making (see pages 16–23).

Body shape A

ARMS
As basic pattern apart from:
Round 6: Work in Black.
Rounds 7–8: Work in Wine Red.
(Work in BLO in round 7.)
Rounds 9–10: Work in Black.
Rounds 11–25: Repeat the pattern, changing colour every 2 rounds to end.

CUFFS
As basic pattern in Black.
Using a length of Black and a needle, sew vertical lines over both the arms to create a check pattern, weaving the needle over the red rounds and under the black rounds.

LEGS
As basic pattern.

BODY & HEAD
As basic pattern apart from:
Rounds 7–8: Work in Black.
Rounds 9–10: Work in Wine Red.
Rounds 11–12: Work in Black.
Rounds 13–27: Repeat the pattern, changing colour every 2 rounds to end. Using a length of Black and a needle, sew vertical lines over body to create a check pattern.

COLLAR
As basic pattern in Wine Red.

Body shape B

ARMS
As basic pattern apart from:
Round 6: Work in Black.
Rounds 7–8: Work in Wine Red.
(Work in BLO in round 7.)
Rounds 9–10: Work in Black.
Rounds 11–22: Repeat the pattern, changing colour every 2 rounds to end.

CUFFS
As basic pattern in Black.
Using a length of Black and a needle, sew vertical lines over both the arms to create a check pattern, weaving the needle over the red rounds and under the black rounds.

LEGS
As basic pattern.

BODY & HEAD
As basic pattern apart from:
Rounds 7–8: Work in Black.
Rounds 9–10: Work in Wine Red.
Rounds 11–12: Work in Black.
Rounds 13–24: Repeat the pattern, changing colour every 2 rounds to end. Using a length of Black and a needle, sew vertical lines over body to create a check pattern.

COLLAR
As basic pattern in Wine Red.

Body shape C

ARMS
As basic pattern apart from:
Rounds 6–7: Work in Black.
(Work in BLO in round 7.)
Rounds 8–9: Work in Wine Red.
Rounds 10–11: Work in Black.
Rounds 12–19: Repeat the pattern, changing colour every 2 rounds to end.

CUFFS
As basic pattern in Black.
Using a length of Black and a needle, sew vertical lines over both the arms to create a check pattern, weaving the needle over the red rounds and under the black rounds.

LEGS
As basic pattern.

BODY & HEAD
As basic pattern apart from:
Rounds 7–8: Work in Black.
Rounds 9–10: Work in Wine Red.
Rounds 11–12: Work in Black.
Rounds 13–20: Repeat the pattern, changing colour every 2 rounds to end. Using a length of Black and a needle, sew vertical lines over body to create a check pattern.

COLLAR
As basic pattern in Wine Red.

Did you know?
There are 60,065 tree species in the world.

Hair

Make Hair Cap on page 24 in Chocolate.

Nose

Sew two small stitches in Skin colour 2 rounds below the eyes.

Beard

Make Long Beard on page 29 in Chocolate.

Braces, optional

Make 2

Ch36 in Red. (Adjust length for different body shapes.) Sl st in 2nd ch from hook and in each st to end.
Fasten off.
Sew one end of each brace to the top of the belt at the front. Pass the brace over the shoulder and cross over at the back and sew in place. You may need a little stitch on the shoulder to keep in place.

Deerstalker hat

Round 1: Using Wine Red, work into a magic ring, 6 dc.

Round 2: 2 dc in each st to end. (12 sts) Change to Black.

Round 3: (2 dc in next st, 1 dc) 6 times. (18 sts)

Round 4: (2 dc in next st, 2 dc) 6 times. (24 sts) Change to Wine Red.

Round 5: (2 dc in next st, 3 dc) 6 times. (30 sts)

Round 6: (2 dc in next st, 4 dc) 6 times. (36 sts) Change to Black.

Round 7: (2 dc in next st, 5 dc) 6 times. (42 sts)

Round 8: (2 dc in next st, 6 dc) 6 times. (48 sts) Change to Wine Red and continue to change colour every 2 rounds.

Rounds 9–16: Dc in each st around. Change to Wine Red. We will now continue in rows.

Row 17: 15 dc, leave remaining sts unworked, turn.

Row 18: Ch1, 30 dc, turn.

Row 19: Ch1, 15 dc, leave remaining sts unworked. Fasten off.

EAR FLAPS
Make 2

Join Black to one corner just created.

Rows 1–2: Ch1, 6 dc, turn. (6 sts) Change to Wine Red and continue the rest of ear flap in the same colour.

Rows 3–4: Ch1, 6 dc, turn. (6 sts)

Row 5: Ch1, dc2tog, 2 dc, dc2tog, turn. (4 sts)

Row 6: Ch1, 2 dc2tog. (2 sts) Fasten off and repeat on the other side. Using a length of Black and a needle, sew vertical lines over the hat to create a check pattern.

Join Light Brown in any st at the back of the hat, dc in each st around the hat, including the rough edges of the flaps, sl st in the first dc to join.

Fasten off and weave in end.

BRIM

Row 1: Ch19 in Light Brown, dc in 2nd ch from hook, dc to end, turn. (18 sts)

Row 2: Dc in each st to end, turn. (18 sts)

Row 3: Ch1, dc2tog, 14 dc, dc2tog, turn. (16 sts)

Row 4: Ch1, dc2tog, 12 dc, dc2tog. (14 sts) Fasten off and sew bottom edge of the brim to the front edge of the hat (there is no need to sew all the way around).

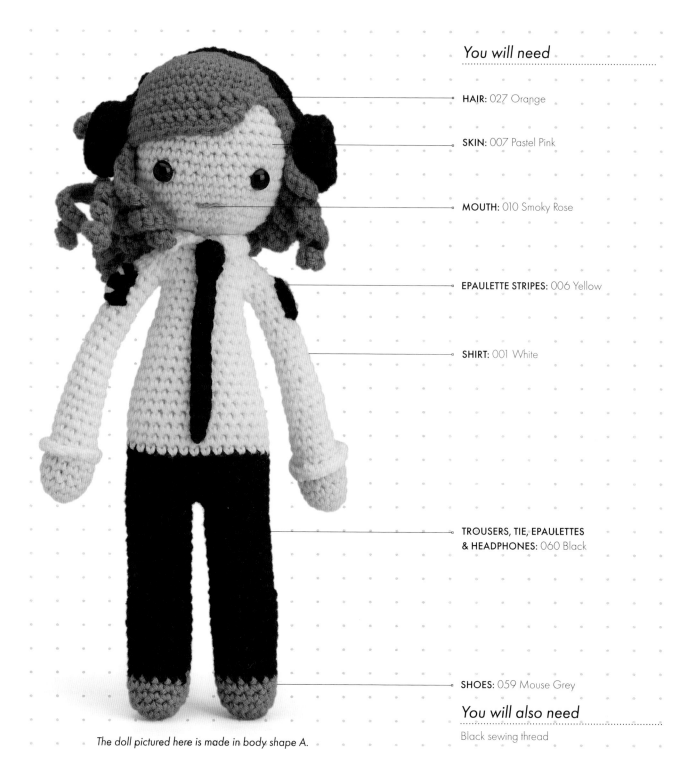

You will need

HAIR: 027 Orange

SKIN: 007 Pastel Pink

MOUTH: 010 Smoky Rose

EPAULETTE STRIPES: 006 Yellow

SHIRT: 001 White

TROUSERS, TIE, EPAULETTES & HEADPHONES: 060 Black

SHOES: 059 Mouse Grey

You will also need

Black sewing thread

The doll pictured here is made in body shape A.

Pilot

After a good night's sleep this pilot arrives at the airport for a flight plan briefing and weather evaluation with the crew before they embark on a long-haul flight to Australia. Once in the cockpit, she checks the technical log then starts to ready the flight deck for departure.

Crochet each part below in order, referring to the body shape you are making (see pages 16–23).

Body shapes A, B & C

ARMS
As basic pattern.

CUFFS
As basic pattern.

LEGS
As basic pattern.

BODY & HEAD
As basic pattern apart from:
Round 8: Do not work in BLO.

COLLAR
As basic pattern.

Hair

Make Long Curly Hair on page 26 in Orange.

Headphones

Make 2

Round 1: Using Black, work into a magic ring, 6 dc.

Round 2: 2 dc in each st to end. (12 sts)

Round 3: (2 dc in next st, 1 dc) 6 times. (18 sts)

Round 4: In BLO dc in each st around.

Rounds 5–6: Dc in each st around.

Sl st and fasten off first earpiece, do not fasten off second earpiece, continue below:

Ch25 (or however many to reach from one earpiece to the other over the head), dc in 2nd ch from hook, dc to end, sl st in next st on earpiece, fasten off.

Join the other end of the head strap to the other earpiece. Weave in ends. Use black sewing thread to sew in place on the hair/head.

Epaulettes

Make 2

Round 1: Ch4 in Black, dc in 2nd ch from hook, 2 dc along rest of ch, turn.

Rounds 2–3: Ch1, 3 dc, turn.

Fasten off leaving a tail.

With Yellow and a tapestry needle, make two large horizontal stitches on each of the arm patches.

Use black sewing thread to sew an arm patch onto the top of each arm.

Tie

Row 1: Ch18 (or however many to reach from the collar to the bottom of the shirt), sl st in 2nd ch from hook, dc in each st to end, fasten off leaving a long tail.

Weave in the starting tail then use the remaining tail to wrap around the top of the tie several times (use a needle to secure it every so often). Use the remaining tail to sew the tie to the neck. Use black sewing thread to sew the bottom on the tie in place.

You will need

HAIR & BEARD: 027 Orange

SKIN: 022 Powder

SHIRT: 001 White

STETHOSCOPE: 006 Black & 059 Mouse Grey

SCRUBS & TROUSERS: 044 Grass Green

BUNNY: 056 Nougat & 002 Cream

SHOES: 060 Black

You will also need

A pair of ¼in (6mm) safety eyes for the bunny (or you can embroider them instead)

The doll pictured here is made in body shape C.

Vet

This vet has a busy clinic today with a wide range of furry and scaly patients to see (one of his favourite's being this giant rabbit). He loves how the job can be so different day to day, seeing a variety of animals with all sorts of care requirements.

Crochet each part below in order, referring to the body shape you are making (see pages 16–23).

Body shapes A, B & C

ARMS
As basic pattern apart from:
Work all rounds in Skin colour.

LEGS
As basic pattern.

BODY & HEAD
As basic pattern apart from:
Round 8: Work in both loops.

Hair

Make Short Curly Hair variation on page 29 and Short Beard on page 29 in Orange.

Scrubs (body shape A)

FRONT PANEL

Row 1: Ch20 in Grass Green, dc in 2nd ch from hook, dc to end of ch, turn. (19 sts)

Rows 2–10: Ch1, dc across, turn. (19 sts)

Row 11: Ch1, dc2tog, 15 dc, dc2tog, turn. (17 sts)

Row 12: Ch1, 17 dc, turn. (17 sts)

Row 13: Ch1, dc2tog, 13 dc, dc2tog, turn. (15 sts)

Row 14: Ch1, 15 dc, turn. (15 sts)

Row 15: Ch1, dc2tog, 11 dc, dc2tog, turn. (13 sts)

Row 16: Ch1, 13 dc, turn. (13 sts)

Row 17: Ch4, dc in 2nd ch from hook, dc along ch, 7 dc, leave rem sts unworked, turn. (10 sts)

Row 18: Ch1, dc2tog, 8 dc, turn. (9 sts)

Row 19: Ch1, 7 dc, dc2tog, turn. (8 sts)

Row 20: Ch1, dc2tog, 6 dc, turn. (7 sts)

Row 21: Ch1, 5 dc, dc2tog, turn. (6 sts)

Row 22: Ch1, dc2tog, 4 dc, turn. (5 sts)

Row 23: Ch1, 3 dc, dc2tog, turn. (4 sts)

Fasten off leaving a long tail for sewing.

Join yarn in the centre st of row 16, you will now work the remaining sts in this row to create the second sleeve:

Row 1: Ch1, 1 dc in same st, 6 dc, turn. (7 sts)

Row 2: Ch4, dc in 2nd ch from hook, dc along ch, 5 dc, dc2tog, turn. (9 sts)

Row 3: Ch1, dc2tog, 7 dc, turn. (8 sts)

Row 4: Ch1, 6 dc, dc2tog, turn. (7 sts)

Row 5: Ch1, dc2tog, 5 dc, turn. (6 sts)

Row 6: Ch1, 4 dc, dc2tog, turn. (5 sts)

Row 7: Ch1, dc2tog, 3 dc, turn. (4 sts)

Row 8: Ch1, 4 dc, turn. (4 sts)

Fasten off leaving a long tail for sewing.

BACK PANEL

Rows 1–16: As front panel.

Row 17: Ch4, dc in 2nd ch from hook, dc along ch, 13 dc, turn. (16 sts)

Row 18: Ch4, dc in 2nd ch from hook, dc along ch, 16 dc, turn. (19 sts)

Rows 19–23: Ch1, dc to end, turn. (19 sts)

Fasten off leaving a long tail for sewing.

Using the tail ends and a mattress st (see page 15), sew the side seams and bottom of the sleeves together. Next, place the scrubs onto the doll. Sew the top sleeve seams when it is on the doll.

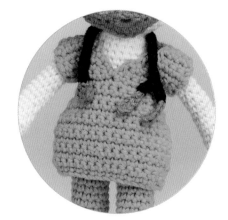

Did you know?
Sir Isaac Newton invented the cat flap. Apparently, he came up with the idea when his cat kept opening the door of his darkened laboratory and ruining his experiments.

Scrubs (body shape B)

FRONT PANEL

Row 1: Ch22 in Grass Green, dc in 2nd ch from hook, dc to end of ch, turn. (21 sts)

Rows 2–12: Ch1, dc across, turn. (21 sts)

Row 13: Ch1, dc2tog, 17 dc, dc2tog, turn. (19 sts)

Row 14: Ch1, dc2tog, 15 dc, dc2tog, turn. (17 sts)

Row 15: Ch1, dc2tog, 13 dc, dc2tog, turn. (15 sts)

Row 16: Ch6, dc in 2nd ch from hook, dc along ch, 8 dc, leave rem sts unworked, turn. (13 sts)

Row 17: Ch1, dc2tog, 11 dc, turn. (12 sts)

Row 18: Ch1, 10 dc, dc2tog, turn. (11 sts)

Row 19: Ch1, dc2tog, 9 dc, turn. (10 sts)

Row 20: Ch1, 8 dc, dc2tog, turn. (9 sts)

Row 21: Ch1, dc2tog, 7 dc, turn. (8 sts)

Row 22: Ch1, 6 dc, dc2tog, turn. (7 sts)

Row 23: Ch1, dc2tog, 5 dc, turn. (6 sts)

Fasten off leaving a long tail for sewing.

Join yarn in the centre st of row 15, you will now work the remaining sts in this row to create the second sleeve:

Row 1: Ch1, 1 dc in same st, 7 dc, turn. (8 sts)

Row 2: Ch6, dc in 2nd ch from hook, dc along ch, 6 dc, dc2tog, turn. (12 sts)

Row 3: Ch1, dc2tog, 10 dc, turn. (11 sts)

Row 4: Ch1, 9 dc, dc2tog, turn. (10 sts)

Row 5: Ch1, dc2tog, 8 dc, turn. (9 sts)

Row 6: Ch1, 7 dc, dc2tog, turn. (8 sts)

Row 7: Ch1, dc2tog, 6 dc, turn. (7 sts)

Row 8: Ch1, 5 dc, dc2tog, turn. (6 sts)

Row 9: Ch1, 6 dc. (6 sts)

Fasten off leaving a long tail for sewing.

BACK PANEL

Rows 1–15: As front panel.

Row 16: Ch6, dc in 2nd ch from hook, dc along ch, 15 dc, turn. (20 sts)

Row 17: Ch6, dc in 2nd ch from hook, dc along ch, 20 dc, turn. (25 sts)

Rows 18–23: Ch1, dc to end, turn. (25 sts)

Fasten off leaving a long tail for sewing.

Using the tail ends and a mattress st (see page 15), sew the side seams and bottom of the sleeves together. Sew the top of one of the sleeves only. Next, place the scrubs onto the doll. Sew the final top sleeve seam when it is on the doll.

Scrubs (body shape C)

FRONT PANEL

Row 1: Ch18 in Grass Green, dc in 2nd ch from hook, dc to end of ch, turn. (17 sts)
Rows 2–7: Ch1, dc across, turn. (17 sts)
Row 8: Ch1, dc2tog, 13 dc, dc2tog, turn. (15 sts)
Row 9: Ch1, 15 dc, turn. (15 sts)
Row 10: Ch1, dc2tog, 11 dc, dc2tog, turn. (13 sts)
Row 11: Ch1, 13 dc, turn. (13 sts)
Row 12: Ch1, dc2tog, 9 dc, dc2tog, turn. (11 sts)
Row 13: Ch1, 11 dc, turn. (11 sts)
Row 14: Ch4, dc in 2nd ch from hook, dc along ch, 6 dc, leave rem sts unworked, turn. (9 sts)
Row 15: Ch1, dc2tog, 7 dc, turn. (8 sts)
Row 16: Ch1, 6 dc, dc2tog, turn. (7 sts)
Row 17: Ch1, dc2tog, 5 dc, turn. (6 sts)
Row 18: Ch1, 4 dc, dc2tog, turn. (5 sts)
Row 19: Ch1, dc2tog, 3 dc, turn. (4 sts)

Fasten off leaving a long tail for sewing. Join yarn in the centre st of row 13, you will now work the remaining sts in this row to create the second sleeve:

Row 1: Ch1, 1 dc in same st, 5 dc, turn. (6 sts)
Row 2: Ch4, dc in 2nd ch from hook, dc along ch, 4 dc, dc2tog, turn. (8 sts)
Row 3: Ch1, dc2tog, 6 dc, turn. (7 sts)
Row 4: Ch1, 5 dc, dc2tog, turn. (6 sts)
Row 5: Ch1, dc2tog, 4 dc, turn. (5 sts)
Row 6: Ch1, 3 dc, dc2tog, turn. (4 sts)
Row 7: Ch1, 4 dc, turn. (4 sts)
Fasten off leaving a long tail for sewing.

BACK PANEL

Rows 1–13: As front panel.
Row 14: Ch4, dc in 2nd ch from hook, dc along ch, 11 dc, turn. (14 sts)
Row 15: Ch4, dc in 2nd ch from hook, dc along ch, 14 dc, turn. (17 sts)
Rows 16–19: Ch1, dc to end, turn. (17 sts)
Fasten off leaving a long tail for sewing.

Using the tail ends and a mattress st (see page 15), sew the side seams and bottom of the sleeves together. Sew the top of one of the sleeves only. Next, place the scrubs onto the doll. Sew the final top sleeve seam when it is on the doll.

Stethoscope

Round 1: Using Mouse Grey, work into a magic ring, 6 dc. (6 sts)
Sl st and fasten off.
Join Black to any st and ch40, sl st in 2nd ch from hook, sl st in next 2 ch, ch4, sl st in 2nd ch from hook, sl st in next 2 ch and along the rest of the initial ch to the bottom, fasten off.
Join Mouse Grey at the end of one of the 'prongs', ch5, 2 dc in 2nd ch from hook, sl st to end. Repeat for second 'prong'.
Weave in all ends.

Bunny

Round 1: Using Nougat, work into a magic ring, 6 dc.
Round 2: 2 dc in each st to end. (12 sts)
Round 3: (2 dc in next st, 1 dc) 6 times. (18 sts)
Round 4: (2 dc in next st, 1 dc) 3 times, 12 dc. (21 sts)
Round 5: (2 dc in next st, 1 dc) 3 times, 15 dc. (24 sts)
Rounds 6–12: Dc in each st around. (24 sts)
Insert safety eyes between rounds 6 and 7.
Round 13: 2 dc, (2 dc in next st, 1 dc) 3 times, 16 dc. (27 sts)
Round 14: Dc in each st around. (27 sts)
Round 15: 3 dc, (2 dc in next st, 2 dc) 3 times, 15 dc. (30 sts)
Rounds 16–20: Dc in each st to end. (30 sts)
Round 21: (Dc2tog, 3 dc) 6 times. (24 sts)
Round 22: (Dc2tog, 2 dc) 6 times. (18 sts)
Round 23: (Dc2tog, 1 dc) 6 times. (12 sts)
Round 24: (Dc2tog) 6 times. (6 sts)
Fasten off. Thread a tapestry needle with the tail end and make some sts to pull the hole closed. Weave in end.

EARS
Make 2
Round 1: Using Nougat, work into a magic ring, 6 dc.
Round 2: 2 dc in each st to end. (12 sts)
Rounds 3–10: Dc in each st around. (12 sts)
Round 11: (Dc2tog, 2 dc) 3 times. (9 sts)
Fasten off leaving a long tail for sewing.
Sew ears to round 11 of body.

TAIL
Round 1: Using Cream, work into a magic ring, 6 dc.
Round 2: 2 dc in each st to end. (12 sts)
Rounds 3–4: Dc in each st around. (12 sts)
Round 5: (Dc2tog) 6 times. (6 sts)
Stuff lightly and sew onto the bunny.

Change the colour of the scrubs for different looks. You could also make him a mask (see Doctor, page 90).

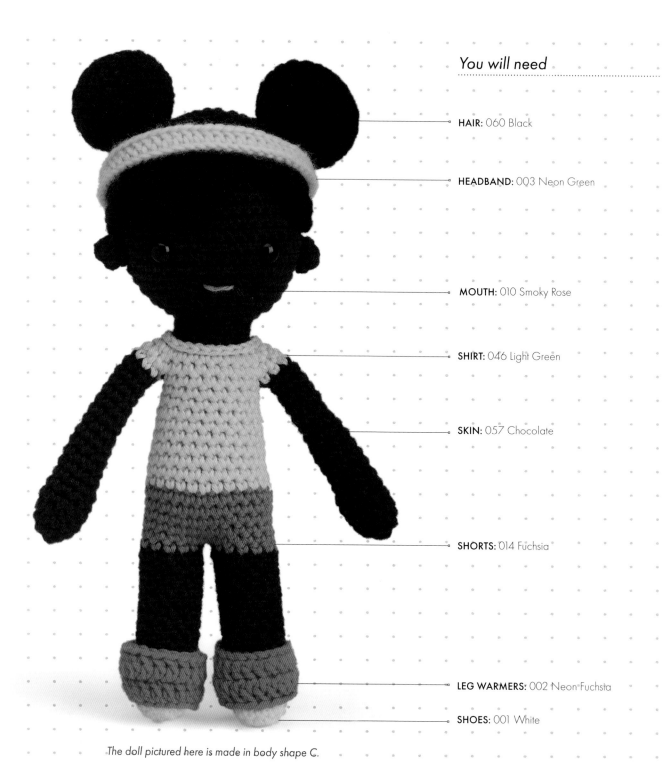

You will need

HAIR: 060 Black

HEADBAND: 003 Neon Green

MOUTH: 010 Smoky Rose

SHIRT: 046 Light Green

SKIN: 057 Chocolate

SHORTS: 014 Fuchsia

LEG WARMERS: 002 Neon Fuchsia

SHOES: 001 White

The doll pictured here is made in body shape C.

Dancer

Starting ballet classes at just three years old, this dancer is now a professional. She has been rehearsing hard all week and today she is auditioning at a studio for a music video. Her dream job would be to dance at one the of big West End shows.

Crochet each part below in order, referring to the body shape you are making (see pages 16–23).

Body shape A

ARMS
As basic pattern apart from:
Work all rounds in Skin colour and do not work in BLO in round 7.

LEGS
As basic pattern apart from:
Round 6 to end: Work all in Skin colour.

BODY & HEAD
As basic pattern apart from:
Round 8: Do not work in BLO.
Round 26: Work in Skin colour in BLO and continue in skin colour to end.

COLLAR
Hold the doll the right way up and insert hook into a FL left in round 25 to the rear of the doll. Sl st in each st to end. Join to the first sl st with another sl st and fasten off. Weave in ends.

EARS
As basic pattern.

Body shape B

ARMS
As basic pattern apart from:
Work all rounds in Skin colour and do not work in BLO in round 7.

LEGS
As basic pattern apart from:
Round 6 to end: Work all in Skin colour.

BODY & HEAD
As basic pattern apart from:
Round 8: Do not work in BLO.
Round 23: Work in Skin colour in BLO and continue in Skin colour to end.

COLLAR
Hold the doll the right way up and insert hook into a FL left in round 22 to the rear of the doll. Sl st in each st to end. Join to the first sl st with another sl st and fasten off. Weave in ends.

EARS
As basic pattern.

Body shape C

ARMS
As basic pattern apart from:
Work all rounds in Skin colour and do not work in BLO in round 7.

LEGS
As basic pattern apart from:
Round 6 to end: Work all in Skin colour.

BODY & HEAD
As basic pattern apart from:
Round 8: Do not work in BLO.
Round 19: Work in Skin colour in BLO and continue in skin colour to end.

COLLAR
Hold the doll the right way up and insert hook into a FL left in round 18 to the rear of the doll. Sl st in each st to end. Join to the first sl st with another sl st and fasten off. Weave in ends.

EARS
As basic pattern.

Hair

Make Double Bun in Black (see pages 27 and 29).

Leg warmers

Make 2
Round 1: Ch20 in Neon Fuchsia, join to first ch with a sl st.
Round 2: Ch3 (counts as 1 tr), 1 tr in each ch around, sl st in the 3rd beg ch to join. (20 sts)
Round 3: Ch3 (counts as 1 tr), 1 tr in each st around, sl st in the 3rd beg ch to join. (20 sts)
Fasten off and weave in ends. Place onto the dancer's ankles.

Headband

Row 1: Ch60 in Neon Green, tr in 4th ch from hook, tr in each ch to end.
Fasten off, sew the two ends together and weave in ends. Place around dancer's head.

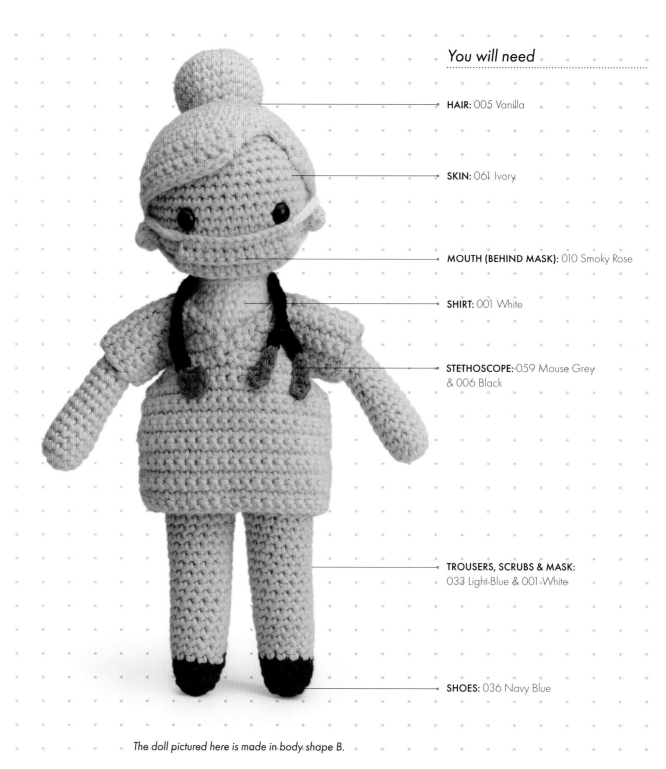

You will need

HAIR: 005 Vanilla

SKIN: 061 Ivory

MOUTH (BEHIND MASK): 010 Smoky Rose

SHIRT: 001 White

STETHOSCOPE: 059 Mouse Grey & 006 Black

TROUSERS, SCRUBS & MASK: 033 Light Blue & 001 White

SHOES: 036 Navy Blue

The doll pictured here is made in body shape B.

Doctor

This doctor is a highly trained neurologist. She treats her patients that have central nervous disorders and she has a busy day ahead of her seeing lots of different people. She prides herself in getting the right diagnoses and helping people get better.

Crochet each part below in order, referring to the body shape you are making (see pages 16–23).

Body shapes A, B & C

ARMS
As basic pattern apart from:
Work all rounds in Skin colour.

LEGS
As basic pattern.

BODY & HEAD
As basic pattern apart from:
Round 8: Work in both loops.

EARS
As basic pattern.

Hair

Make Bun on page 27 in Vanilla.

Scrubs (body shape A)

FRONT PANEL

Row 1: Ch20 in Light Blue, dc in 2nd ch from hook, dc to end of ch, turn. (19 sts)

Rows 2–10: Ch1, dc across, turn. (19 sts)

Row 11: Ch1, dc2tog, 15 dc, dc2tog, turn. (17 sts)

Row 12: Ch1, 17 dc, turn. (17 sts)

Row 13: Ch1, dc2tog, 13 dc, dc2tog, turn. (15 sts)

Row 14: Ch1, 15 dc, turn. (15 sts)

Row 15: Ch1, dc2tog, 11 dc, dc2tog, turn. (13 sts)

Row 16: Ch1, 13 dc, turn. (13 sts)

Row 17: Ch4, dc in 2nd ch from hook, dc along ch, 7 dc, leave rem sts unworked, turn. (10 sts)

Row 18: Ch1, dc2tog, 8 dc, turn. (9 sts)

Row 19: Ch1, 7 dc, dc2tog, turn. (8 sts)

Row 20: Ch1, dc2tog, 6 dc, turn. (7 sts)

Row 21: Ch1, 5 dc, dc2tog, turn. (6 sts)

Row 22: Ch1, dc2tog, 4 dc, turn. (5 sts)

Row 23: Ch1, 3 dc, dc2tog, turn. (4 sts)

Fasten off leaving a long tail for sewing.

Join yarn in the centre st of row 16, you will now work the remaining sts in this row to create the second sleeve:

Row 1: Ch1, 1 dc in same st, 6 dc, turn. (7 sts)

Row 2: Ch4, dc in 2nd ch from hook, dc along ch, 5 dc, dc2tog, turn. (9 sts)

Row 3: Ch1, dc2tog, 7 dc, turn. (8 sts)

Row 4: Ch1, 6 dc, dc2tog, turn. (7 sts)

Row 5: Ch1, dc2tog, 5 dc, turn. (6 sts)

Row 6: Ch1, 4 dc, dc2tog, turn. (5 sts)

Row 7: Ch1, dc2tog, 3 dc, turn. (4 sts)

Row 8: Ch1, 4 dc, turn. (4 sts)

Fasten off leaving a long tail for sewing.

BACK PANEL

Rows 1–16: As front panel.

Row 17: Ch4, dc in 2nd ch from hook, dc along ch, 13 dc, turn. (16 sts)

Row 18: Ch4, dc in 2nd ch from hook, dc along ch, 16 dc, turn. (19 sts)

Rows 19–23: Ch1, dc to end, turn. (19 sts)

Fasten off leaving a long tail for sewing.

Using the tail ends and a mattress st (see page 15), sew the side seams and bottom of the sleeves together. Next, place the scrubs onto the doll. Sew the top sleeve seams when it is on the doll.

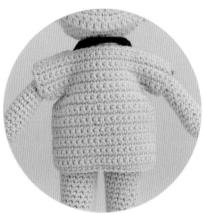

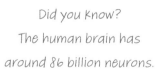

Did you Know?
The human brain has
around 86 billion neurons.

Scrubs (body shape B)

FRONT PANEL

Row 1: Ch22 in Light Blue, dc in 2nd ch from hook, dc to end of ch, turn. (21 sts)

Rows 2–12: Ch1, dc across, turn. (21 sts)

Row 13: Ch1, dc2tog, 17 dc, dc2tog, turn. (19 sts)

Row 14: Ch1, dc2tog, 15 dc, dc2tog, turn. (17 sts)

Row 15: Ch1, dc2tog, 13 dc, dc2tog, turn. (15 sts)

Row 16: Ch6, dc in 2nd ch from hook, dc along ch, 8 dc, leave rem sts unworked, turn. (13 sts)

Row 17: Ch1, dc2tog, 11 dc, turn. (12 sts)

Row 18: Ch1, 10 dc, dc2tog, turn. (11 sts)

Row 19: Ch1, dc2tog, 9 dc, turn. (10 sts)

Row 20: Ch1, 8 dc, dc2tog, turn. (9 sts)

Row 21: Ch1, dc2tog, 7 dc, turn. (8 sts)

Row 22: Ch1, 6 dc, dc2tog, turn. (7 sts)

Row 23: Ch1, dc2tog, 5 dc, turn. (6 sts)

Fasten off leaving a long tail for sewing.

Join yarn in the centre st of row 15, you will now work the remaining sts in this row to create the second sleeve:

Row 1: Ch1, 1 dc in same st, 7 dc, turn. (8 sts)

Row 2: Ch6, dc in 2nd ch from hook, dc along ch, 6 dc, dc2tog, turn. (12 sts)

Row 3: Ch1, dc2tog, 10 dc, turn. (11 sts)

Row 4: Ch1, 9 dc, dc2tog, turn. (10 sts)

Row 5: Ch1, dc2tog, 8 dc, turn. (9 sts)

Row 6: Ch1, 7 dc, dc2tog, turn. (8 sts)

Row 7: Ch1, dc2tog, 6 dc, turn. (7 sts)

Row 8: Ch1, 5 dc, dc2tog, turn. (6 sts)

Row 9: Ch1, 6 dc. (6 sts)

Fasten off leaving a long tail for sewing.

BACK PANEL

Rows 1–15: As front panel.

Row 16: Ch6, dc in 2nd ch from hook, dc along ch, 15 dc, turn. (20 sts)

Row 17: Ch6, dc in 2nd ch from hook, dc along ch, 20 dc, turn. (25 sts)

Rows 18–23: Ch1, dc to end, turn. (25 sts)

Fasten off leaving a long tail for sewing.

Using the tail ends and a mattress st (see page 15), sew the side seams and bottom of the sleeves together. Next, place the scrubs onto the doll. Sew the top sleeve seams when it is on the doll.

Scrubs (body shape C)

FRONT PANEL

Row 1: Ch18 in Light Blue, dc in 2nd ch from hook, dc to end of ch, turn. (17 sts)

Rows 2–7: Ch1, dc across, turn. (17 sts)

Row 8: Ch1, dc2tog, 13 dc, dc2tog, turn. (15 sts)

Row 9: Ch1, 15 dc, turn. (15 sts)

Row 10: Ch1, dc2tog, 11 dc, dc2tog, turn. (13 sts)

Row 11: Ch1, 13 dc, turn. (13 sts)

Row 12: Ch1, dc2tog, 9 dc, dc2tog, turn. (11 sts)

Row 13: Ch1, 11 dc, turn. (11 sts)

Row 14: Ch4, dc in 2nd ch from hook, dc along ch, 6 dc, leave rem sts unworked, turn. (9 sts)

Row 15: Ch1, dc2tog, 7 dc, turn. (8 sts)

Row 16: Ch1, 6 dc, dc2tog, turn. (7 sts)

Row 17: Ch1, dc2tog, 5 dc, turn. (6 sts)

Row 18: Ch1, 4 dc, dc2tog, turn. (5 sts)

Row 19: Ch1, dc2tog, 3 dc, turn. (4 sts)

Fasten off leaving a long tail for sewing. Join yarn in the centre st of row 13, you will now work the remaining sts in this row to create the second sleeve:

Row 1: Ch1, 1 dc in same st, 5 dc, turn. (6 sts)

Row 2: Ch4, dc in 2nd ch from hook, dc along ch, 4 dc, dc2tog, turn. (8 sts)

Row 3: Ch1, dc2tog, 6 dc, turn. (7 sts)

Row 4: Ch1, 5 dc, dc2tog, turn. (6 sts)

Row 5: Ch1, dc2tog, 4 dc, turn. (5 sts)

Row 6: Ch1, 3 dc, dc2tog, turn. (4 sts)

Row 7: Ch1, 4 dc, turn. (4 sts)

Fasten off leaving a long tail for sewing.

BACK PANEL

Rows 1–13: As front panel.

Row 14: Ch4, dc in 2nd ch from hook, dc along ch, 11 dc, turn. (14 sts)

Row 15: Ch4, dc in 2nd ch from hook, dc along ch, 14 dc, turn. (17 sts)

Rows 16–19: Ch1, dc to end, turn. (17 sts)

Fasten off leaving a long tail for sewing.

Using the tail ends and a mattress st (see page 15), sew the side seams and bottom of the sleeves together. Next, place the scrubs onto the doll. Sew the top sleeve seams when it is on the doll.

Mask

Row 1: Ch 13 in Light Blue, dc in 2nd ch from hook, dc to end. (12 sts)
Rows 2–6: In BLO, dc to end. (12 sts)
Fasten off and weave in ends.

MASK STRAPS
Make 2
Ch 13 in White (adjust as necessary to suit your doll), fasten off and sew to the corners of the mask.
Wrap the straps around the ears. If your doll does not have ears, then you can make the straps longer to wrap around the head.

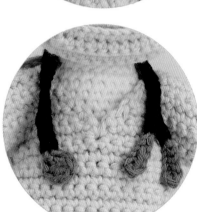

Stethoscope

Round 1: Using Mouse Grey, work into a magic ring, 6 dc. (6 sts)
Sl st and fasten off.
Join Black to any st and ch40, sl st in 2nd ch from hook, sl st in next 2 ch, ch4, sl st in 2nd ch from hook, sl st in next 2 ch and along the rest of the initial ch to the bottom, fasten off.
Join Mouse Grey at the end of one of the 'prongs', ch5, 2 dc in 2nd ch from hook, sl st to end. Fasten off. Repeat for second 'prong'.
Weave in all ends.

Change the colour of the scrubs for a different look. The stethoscope could also be sewn in place.

HAT: 071 Sand

SKIN: 053 Caramel

MOUTH: 010 Smoky Rose

HAIR: 005 Vanilla

SHIRT: 033 Light Blue

DUNGAREES: 034 Denim

BOOTS: 048 Olive

The doll pictured here is made in body shape C.

Farmer

Early mornings are part of the job for this farmer; she's been up since 5.30am to feed and milk the cows. The best thing about being up so early is seeing the sun rise and being in the countryside when it's so still and quiet.

Crochet each part below in order, referring to the body shape you are making (see pages 16–23).

Body shape A

ARMS
As basic pattern.

CUFFS
As basic pattern.

LEGS
As basic pattern apart from:
Rounds 1–12: Work in Olive.
Rounds 13–26: Work in Denim.

BODY & HEAD
As basic pattern apart from:
Rounds 7–22: Do not change to shirt colour, continue in Denim.
Round 8: Do not work in BLO.
Rounds 23–27: Work in Light Blue.

COLLAR
As basic pattern.

Body shape B

ARMS
As basic pattern.

CUFFS
As basic pattern.

LEGS
As basic pattern apart from:
Rounds 1–11: Work in Olive.
Rounds 12–22: Work in Denim.

BODY & HEAD
As basic pattern apart from:
Rounds 7–19: Do not change to shirt colour, continue in Denim.
Round 8: Do not work in BLO.
Rounds 20–24: Work in Light Blue.

COLLAR
As basic pattern.

Body shape C

ARMS
As basic pattern.

CUFFS
As basic pattern.

LEGS
As basic pattern apart from:
Rounds 1–10: Work in Olive.
Rounds 11–19: Work in Denim.

BODY & HEAD
As basic pattern apart from:
Rounds 7–15: Do not change to shirt colour, continue in Denim.
Round 8: Do not work in BLO.
Rounds 16–20: Work in Light Blue.

COLLAR
As basic pattern.

Hair

Make Long Curly Hair on page 26 in Vanilla.

Hat

Round 1: Using Sand, work into a magic ring, 6 dc.
Round 2: 2 dc in each st to end. (12 sts)
Round 3: (2 dc in next st, 1 dc) 6 times. (18 sts)
Round 4: (2 dc in next st, 2 dc) 6 times. (24 sts)
Round 5: (2 dc in next st, 3 dc) 6 times. (30 sts)
Round 6: (2 dc in next st, 4 dc) 6 times. (36 sts)
Round 7: (2 dc in next st, 5 dc) 6 times. (42 sts)
Round 8: (2 dc in next st, 6 dc) 6 times. (48 sts)
Rounds 9: In BLO dc in each st around. (48 sts)
Rounds 10–14: Dc in each st to end.
Round 15: 4 dc, (2 dc in next st, 7 dc) 5 times, 2 dc in next st, 3 dc. (54 sts)
Round 16: (2 dc in next st, 8 dc) 6 times. (60 sts)
Round 17: 5 dc, (2 dc in next st, 9 dc) 5 times, 2 dc in next st, 4 dc. (66 sts)
Round 18: (2 dc in next st, 10 dc) 6 times. (72 sts)
Sl st into next st to close spiral.
Fasten off and weave in ends.

Shoulder straps

Make 2
Ch 16 in Denim. (Adjust length for different body shapes.) Sl st in 2nd ch from hook and in each st to end.
Fasten off.
Sew one end of each strap to the top of the dungarees at the front. Pass the brace over the shoulder sew in place at the back. You may need a little stitch on the shoulder to keep in place.

> Did you know?
> Pizza farms are places, mainly in the US, where farmers grow and produce everything needed to make pizzas.

HAIR: 056 Nougat

SKIN: 065 Blush

MOUTH: 010 Smoky Rose

SHIRT: 042 Emerald

RACE NUMBER & SHOELACES:
060 Black

SHORTS: 036 Navy Blue

**SHOES, HEADBAND,
ARMBAND & NUMBER BIB:**
001 White

The doll pictured here is made in body shape C.

Athlete

Training for athletes is hard work – there are early starts six days week. This athlete is making sure her body is in peak condition for the Olympics coming up soon. She takes part in the high jump competition, so has been perfecting her Fosbury Flop.

Crochet each part below in order, referring to the body shape you are making (see pages 16–23).

Body shapes A, B & C

ARMS
As basic pattern apart from:
Work all rounds in Skin colour and do not work in BLO in round 7.

LEGS
As basic pattern apart from:
Round 6 to end: Work all in Skin colour.

BODY & HEAD
As basic pattern apart from:
Round 8: Do not work in BLO.

EARS
As basic pattern.

Hair

Make Long Hair on page 28 in Nougat.
Tie in a ponytail with the same-coloured yarn.

Shoes

Using Navy Blue sew two small stitches on the front of each shoe for laces.

Number bib

Row 1: Ch9 in White, dc in 2nd ch from hook, dc in each ch to end, turn. (8 sts)
Rows 2–5: Ch1, 8 dc, turn. (8 sts)
Fasten off and weave in ends.
Use Black and a needle to sew on some numbers.

Headband

Row 1: Ch55 (or however many to wrap around the head) in White, dc in 2nd ch from hook, dc in each ch to end.
Fasten off, sew the two ends together and weave in ends. Place around Athlete's head.

Armband

Row 1: Ch16 (or however many to wrap around the arm) in White, dc in 2nd ch from hook, dc in each ch to end.
Fasten off, sew the two ends together and weave in ends. Place on Athlete's arm.

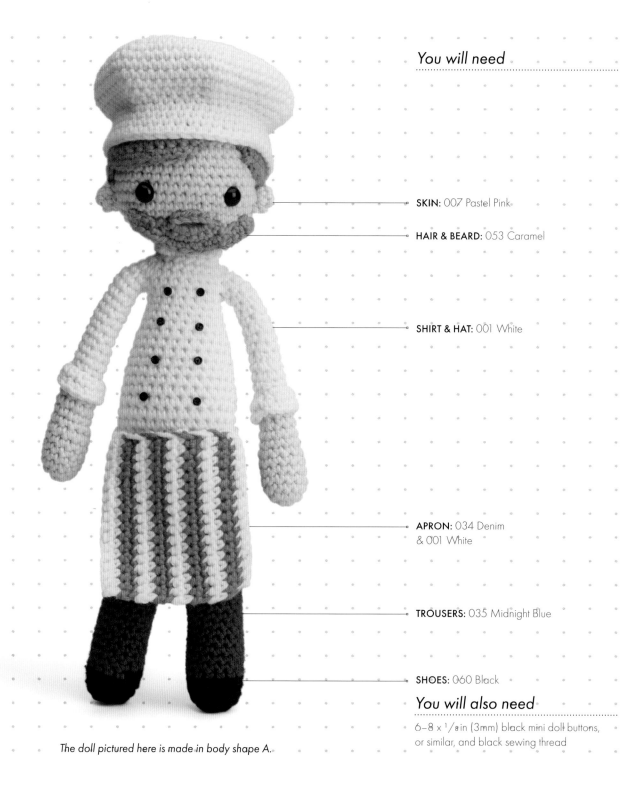

SKIN: 007 Pastel Pink

HAIR & BEARD: 053 Caramel

SHIRT & HAT: 001 White

APRON: 034 Denim & 001 White

TROUSERS: 035 Midnight Blue

SHOES: 060 Black

You will also need

6–8 x ¹/₈ in (3mm) black mini doll buttons, or similar, and black sewing thread

The doll pictured here is made in body shape A.

Chef

This chef has recently opened his first restaurant and it has been a complete success. Specializing in food sourced from good-quality locally grown produce the 5-star reviews are flooding in. His signature dish is seared scallops with pea puree, chorizo and capers.

Crochet each part below in order, referring to the body shape you are making (see pages 16–23).

Body shape A

ARMS
As basic pattern apart from:
Rounds 1–12: Work in Skin colour. (Do not work in BLO in round 7.)
Rounds 13–25: Work in White, working in BLO in round 14.

CUFFS
Holding arm upside down join White to a FL left in round 13.
Round 1: (2 dc in next st, 4 dc) twice. (12 sts)
Round 2: (2 dc in next st, 5 dc) twice. (14 sts)
Fasten off and weave in ends.

LEGS
As basic pattern.

BODY & HEAD
As basic pattern.

BOTTOM OF JACKET
Hold doll upside down and join White to a FL left in round 7. Ch1 and dc around. Sl st into the first dc. Fasten off and weave in ends.

COLLAR
Hold doll the right way up and join White to a FL left in round 27 (into the second st to the right of the centre front). Ch1, 14 dc, leave remaining 2 sts unworked. Fasten off and weave in ends. You should have a collar with a gap of 2 sts in the centre.

EARS
As basic pattern.

Body shape B

ARMS
As basic pattern apart from:
Rounds 1–11: Work in Skin colour. (Do not work in BLO in round 7.)
Rounds 12–22: Work in White, working in BLO in round 13.

CUFFS
Holding arm upside down join White to a FL left in round 12.
Round 1: (2 dc in next st, 4 dc) twice. (12 sts)
Round 2: (2 dc in next st, 5 dc) twice. (14 sts)
Fasten off and weave in ends.

LEGS
As basic pattern.

BODY & HEAD
As basic pattern.

BOTTOM OF JACKET
Hold doll upside down and join White to a FL left in round 7. Ch1 and dc around. Sl st into the first dc. Fasten off and weave in ends.

COLLAR
Hold doll the right way up and join White to a FL left in round 24 (into the second st to the right of the centre front). Ch1, 16 dc, leave remaining 2 sts unworked. Fasten off and weave in ends. You should have a collar with a gap of 2 sts in the centre.

EARS
As basic pattern.

Body shape C

ARMS
As basic pattern apart from:
Rounds 1–9: Work in Skin colour. (Do not work in BLO in round 7.)
Rounds 10–19: Work in White working in BLO in round 11.

CUFFS
Holding arm upside down join White to a FL left in round 10.
Round 1: (2 dc in next st, 3 dc) twice, 1 dc. (11 sts)
Round 2: (2 dc in next st, 4 dc) twice, 1 dc. (13 sts)
Fasten off and weave in ends.

LEGS
As basic pattern.

BODY & HEAD
As basic pattern.

BOTTOM OF JACKET
Hold doll upside down and join White to a FL left in round 7. Ch1 and dc around. Sl st into the first dc. Fasten off and weave in ends.

COLLAR
Hold doll the right way up and join White to a FL left in round 20 (into the second st to the right of the centre front). Ch1, 16 dc, leave remaining 2 sts unworked. Fasten off and weave in ends. You should have a collar with a gap of 2 sts in the centre.

EARS
As basic pattern.

Hair

Make Hair Cap on page 24 in Caramel.

Beard

Make Short Beard on page 29 in Caramel.

Apron

Row 1: Ch 17 for body shapes A and B, Ch 13 for body shape C in White leaving a long starting tail, 1 dc in 2nd ch from hook, dc to end, turn.

Row 2: Ch 1, dc to end, turn.
Change to Denim.

Rows 3–4: Ch 1, dc to end, turn.
Change to White.

Rows 5–6: Ch 1, dc to end, turn.
Change to Denim.

Rows 7–8: Ch 1, dc to end, turn.
Change to White.

Rows 9–10: Ch 1, dc to end, turn.
Change to Denim.

Rows 11–12: Ch 1, dc to end, turn.
Change to White.

Rows 13–14: Ch 1, dc to end, turn.
Change to Denim.

Rows 15–16: Ch 1, dc to end, turn.
Change to White.

Rows 17–18: Ch 1, dc to end, turn.
Fasten off leaving long tail, use this and the starting tail as the apron ties.

Chef's hat

Round 1: Using White, work into a magic ring, 6 dc. (6 sts)

Round 2: 2 dc in each st to end. (12 sts)

Round 3: (2 dc in next st, 1 dc) 6 times. (18 sts)

Round 4: (2 dc in next st, 2 dc) 6 times. (24 sts)

Round 5: (2 dc in next st, 3 dc) 6 times. (30 sts)

Round 6: (2 dc in next st, 4 dc) 6 times. (36 sts)

Round 7: (2 dc in next st, 5 dc) 6 times. (42 sts)

Round 8: (2 dc in next st, 6 dc) 6 times. (48 sts)

Round 9: (2 dc in next st, 7 dc) 6 times. (54 sts)

Round 10: (2 dc in next st, 8 dc) 6 times. (60 sts)

Rounds 11–14: Dc in each st around.

Round 15: (Dc2tog, 8 dc) 6 times. (54 sts)

Round 16: (Dc2tog, 7 dc) 6 times. (48 sts)

Round 17: (Dc2tog, 6 dc) 6 times. (42 sts)

Rounds 18–20: Dc in each st around.
Sl st to close spiral. Fasten off and weave in end.

Did you know?
The fear of getting peanut butter stuck to the roof of your mouth is called arachibutyrophobia.

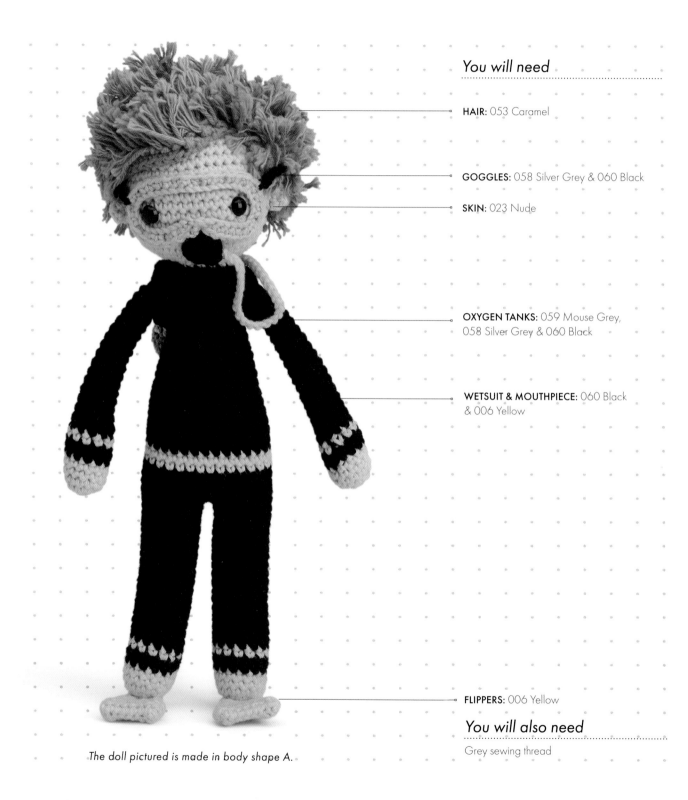

HAIR: 053 Caramel

GOGGLES: 058 Silver Grey & 060 Black

SKIN: 023 Nude

OXYGEN TANKS: 059 Mouse Grey, 058 Silver Grey & 060 Black

WETSUIT & MOUTHPIECE: 060 Black & 006 Yellow

FLIPPERS: 006 Yellow

You will also need

Grey sewing thread

The doll pictured is made in body shape A.

Diver

This diver is getting ready to take a new class scuba diving off the coast of Indonesia. The variety of sea life is exceptional and diving here never gets boring. Today he hopes to see some manta rays, turtles and whale sharks.

Crochet each part below in order, referring to the body shape you are making (see pages 16–23).

Body shapes A, B & C

ARMS
As basic pattern apart from:
Round 7: Do not work into BLO.
Round 8: Work in Yellow.
Do not make the cuffs.

LEGS
As basic pattern apart from:
Round 8: Work in Yellow.

BODY & HEAD
As basic pattern apart from:
Rounds 6 & 7: Work in Yellow.
Round 8: Do not work in BLO.
Do not add stitch for mouth.

EARS
As basic pattern.

Hair

Make Short Hair on page 25 in Caramel.

Oxygen tanks

Make 2
Round 1: Using Mouse Grey, work into a magic ring, 6 dc.
Round 2: 2 dc in each st around. (12 sts)
Round 3: Dc around in BLO. (12 sts)
Rounds 4–5: Dc in each st around. (12 sts)
Change to Silver Grey. Stuff as you go.
Rounds 6–12: Dc in each st around. (12 sts)
Round 13: (Dc2tog) 6 times. (6 sts)
Change to Mouse Grey.
Round 14: Dc in each st around. (6 sts)
Fasten off leaving a tail and use this to sew through the last round to close the hole.

TANK STRAP

Row 1: Ch3 in Black, 1 dc in 2nd ch from hook, 1 dc, turn. (2 sts)
Row 2: Ch1, 2 dc, turn.
Fasten off, wrap around the tanks and use the tail end to sew in place. Weave in end.

SHOULDER STRAPS
Make 2
Row 1: Ch15 in Black, 1 dc in 2nd ch from hook, 13 dc along rest of ch. (14 sts)
Fasten off.
Sew one end of the strap onto the top edge of the tank strap. Sew the other end onto round 13 of the oxygen tank. Repeat with other strap.
Pass each arm though a strap to place onto the back.
You may need to adjust the length of the initial ch to fit your doll.

Mouthpiece

Round 1: Using Black, work into a magic ring, 6 dc.
Round 2: 2 dc in each st to end. (12 sts)
Sl st in next st to close spiral, fasten off.
Sew onto face.

Using Yellow, ch30 approx. (enough to reach from the mouthpiece around to the top of the oxygen tanks on the back). Sew one end of the ch on the edge of the mouthpiece and the other on top of one of the oxygen tanks.

Goggles

Row 1: Ch41 in Silver Grey, dc in 2nd ch from hook, 39 dc along the rest of ch.
Fasten off and weave in ends. Pin in place around the eyes and over the mouthpiece. Use a similar coloured sewing thread to sew into place.

GOGGLE STRAP

Ch40 in Black (or enough to stretch around head), sew each end onto the sides of the goggles.

Flippers

Make 2
Round 1: Ch9 in Yellow, 1 dc in 2nd ch from hook, dc to end, working on the other side of the ch, dc to end. (16 sts)
Round 2: Dc in each st around.
Round 3: (Dc2tog, 6 dc) 2 times. (14 sts)
Round 4: Dc in each st around. (14 sts)
Round 5: (Dc2tog, 5 dc) 2 times. (12 sts)
Round 6: Dc in each st around. (12 sts)
Round 7: (Dc2tog, 4 dc) 2 times. (10 sts)
Round 8: Dc in each st around. (10 sts)
Fasten off leaving a long tail and sew onto the bottom of the feet.

Did you know?
Scuba stands for 'Self-contained underwater breathing apparatus'.

You will need

HAIR: 056 Nougat

MOUTH: 010 Smoky Rose

BACKPACK: 057 Chocolate & 052 Light Brown

SHIRT: 077 Pea

GILET: 025 Fox

SKIN: 023 Nude

TROUSERS & HAT: 048 Olive

SHOES & BELT: 057 Chocolate

The doll pictured here is made in body shape C.

Explorer

Exploring 'in the field' rather than at a desk is definitely the highlight of the job for this anthropologist. She is getting ready for an expedition to the Himalayas. Attention to detail and a taste of adventure are key skills in this field, which she has plenty of.

Crochet each part below in order, referring to the body shape you are making (see pages 16–23).

Body shapes A, B & C

ARMS
As basic pattern apart from:
Round 7: Do not work in BLO.

LEGS
As basic pattern.

BODY & HEAD
As basic pattern apart from:
Round 7: Work in Chocolate.

Hair

Make Hair Cap on page 24 in Nougat. Add hair to hair cap (see page 25) in the bottom 2 rounds only in Light Brown. Trim to desired length, cut a fringe above right eye.

Gilet (body shape A)

Note: To create the ridged texture, work in BLO throughout.
Row 1: Ch39 in Fox, dc in 2nd ch from hook, dc to end of ch, turn. (38 sts)
Rows 2–14: Ch1, dc across, turn. (38 sts)
Row 15: Ch1, 10 dc, leave rem sts unworked, turn. (10 sts)
Rows 16–18: Ch1, 10 dc, turn. (10 sts)
Row 19: Ch1, dc2tog, 8 dc, turn. (9 sts)
Row 20: Ch1, 7 dc, dc2tog, turn. (8 sts)
Row 21: Ch1, dc2tog, 4 dc, dc2tog. (6 sts)
Fasten off. Join yarn in the next st on main panel from panel just made.

Rows 1–6: Ch1, 18 dc, turn. (18 sts)
Row 7: Ch1, dc2tog, 14 dc, dc2tog, turn. (16 sts)
Fasten off. Join yarn in the next st on main panel from panel just made.

Rows 1–4: Ch1, 10 dc, turn. (10 sts)
Row 5: Ch1, 8 dc, dc2tog, turn. (9 sts)
Row 6: Ch1, dc2tog, 7 dc, turn. (8 sts)
Row 7: Ch1, dc2tog, 4 dc, dc2tog. (6 sts)
Fasten off.
Fold the side panels in and use the tail end to sew the top of the front panels to the top corners of the back panel. Weave in ends.

Gilet (body shape B)

Note: To create the ridged texture, work in BLO throughout.
Row 1: Ch47 in Fox, dc in 2nd ch from hook, dc to end of ch, turn. (46 sts)
Rows 2–12: Ch1, dc across, turn. (46 sts)
Row 13: Ch1, 12 dc, leave rem sts unworked, turn. (12 sts)
Rows 14–15: Ch1, 12 dc, turn. (12 sts)
Row 16: Ch1, 10 dc, dc2tog, turn. (11 sts)
Row 17: Ch1, dc2tog, 9 dc turn. (10 sts)
Row 18: Ch1, dc2tog, 6 dc, dc2tog. (8 sts)
Row 19: Ch1, dc2tog, 4 dc, dc2tog. (6 sts)
Fasten off. Join yarn in the next st on main panel from panel just made.

Rows 1–4: Ch1, 22 dc, turn. (22 sts)
Row 5: Ch1, dc2tog, 18 dc, dc2tog, turn. (20 sts)
Row 6: Ch1, dc2tog, 16 dc, dc2tog, turn. (18 sts)
Row 7: Ch1, dc2tog, 14 dc, dc2tog, turn. (16 sts)
Fasten off. Join yarn in the next st on main panel from panel just made.

Rows 1–3: Ch1, 12 dc, turn. (12sts)
Row 4: Ch1, dc2tog, 10 dc, turn. (11 sts)
Row 5: Ch1, 9 dc, dc2tog, turn. (10 sts)
Row 6: Ch1, dc2tog, 6 dc, dc2tog. (8 sts)
Row 7: Ch1, dc2tog, 4 dc, dc2tog. (6 sts)
Fasten off.
Fold the side panels in and use the tail end to sew the top of the front panels to the top corners of the back panel. Weave in ends.

Did you know?
Cartographers (mapmakers) would often include fake towns, know as 'paper towns' in their maps so they could easily spot if others had copied their map.

Gilet (body shape C)

Note: To create the ridged texture, work in BLO throughout.

Row 1: Ch35 in Fox, dc in 2nd ch from hook, dc to end of ch, turn. (34 sts)

Rows 2–10: Ch1, dc across, turn. (34 sts)

Row 11: Ch1, 9 dc, leave rem sts unworked, turn. (9 sts)

Rows 12–13: Ch1, 9 dc, turn. (9 sts)

Row 14: Ch1, 7 dc, dc2tog, turn. (8 sts)

Row 15: Ch1, dc2tog, 6 dc, turn. (7 sts)

Row 16: Ch1, dc2tog, 3 dc, dc2tog. (5 sts)

Fasten off. Join yarn in the next st on main panel from panel just made.

Rows 1–5: Ch1, 16 dc, turn. (16 sts)

Row 6: Ch1, dc2tog, 12 dc, dc2tog, turn. (14 sts)

Fasten off. Join yarn in the next st on main panel from panel just made.

Rows 1–3: Ch1, 9 dc, turn. (9 sts)

Row 4: Ch1, dc2tog, 7 dc, turn. (8 sts)

Row 5: Ch1, 6 dc, dc2tog, turn. (7 sts)

Row 6: Ch1, dc2tog, 3 dc, dc2tog. (5 sts)

Fasten off.

Fold the side panels in and use the tail end to sew the top of the front panels to the top corners of the back panel. Weave in ends.

Hat

Round 1: Using Olive, work into a magic ring, 6 dc.

Round 2: 2 dc in each st to end. (12 sts)

Round 3: (2 dc in next st, 1 dc) 6 times. (18 sts)

Round 4: (2 dc in next st, 2 dc) 6 times. (24 sts)

Round 5: (2 dc in next st, 3 dc) 6 times. (30 sts)

Round 6: (2 dc in next st, 4 dc) 6 times. (36 sts)

Round 7: (2 dc in next st, 5 dc) 6 times. (42 sts)

Rounds 8–15: Dc in each st around.

Fasten off and weave in ends.

BRIM

Row 1: Ch5 in Olive, dc in 2nd ch from hook, dc to end, turn. (4 sts)

Rows 2–48: Ch1, 4 dc in BLO, turn. (4 sts). Adjust number of rows to fit around the hat/head.

Fasten off and use the tail end to sew the brim to the hat. Weave in any remaining ends.

Backpack

Round 1: Ch11 in Chocolate, 2 dc in 2nd ch from hook, 8 dc, 2 dc in next st, working on the other side of the ch, 2 dc in same st, 8 dc, 2 dc in next st. (24 sts)

Rounds 2–3: Dc in each st around. (24 sts) Change to Light Brown.

Rounds 4–12: Dc in each st around. (24 sts)

Round 13: (Dc2tog, 10 dc) 2 times. (22 sts)

Round 14: (Dc2tog, 9 dc) 2 times. (20 sts)

Now, continue in rows to form the top of the bag.

1 dc (or however many required to reach the side of the bag).

Row 15: Turn, ch1, 9 dc, turn. (9 sts)

Rows 16–17: Ch1, 9 dc, turn. (9 sts)

Row 18: Dc2tog, 5 dc, dc2tog. (7 sts) Fasten off.

Join Chocolate to the right-hand side of the flap and dc along the edge.

Stuff and sew the flap down.

FRONT STRAPS
Make 2

Row 1: Ch5 in Chocolate, dc in 2nd ch from hook, 3 dc. (4 sts)
Fasten off.

Sew onto the front of the bag flap. Using a tapestry needle and Light Brown, sew two small sts to secure the ends of the straps to the bag.

SHOULDER STRAPS
Make 2

Row 1: Ch20 (or however many needed to loop over arms) in Chocolate, dc in 2nd ch from hook, dc in each ch to end. (19 sts)
Fasten off and sew onto the bag.
Weave in all ends.

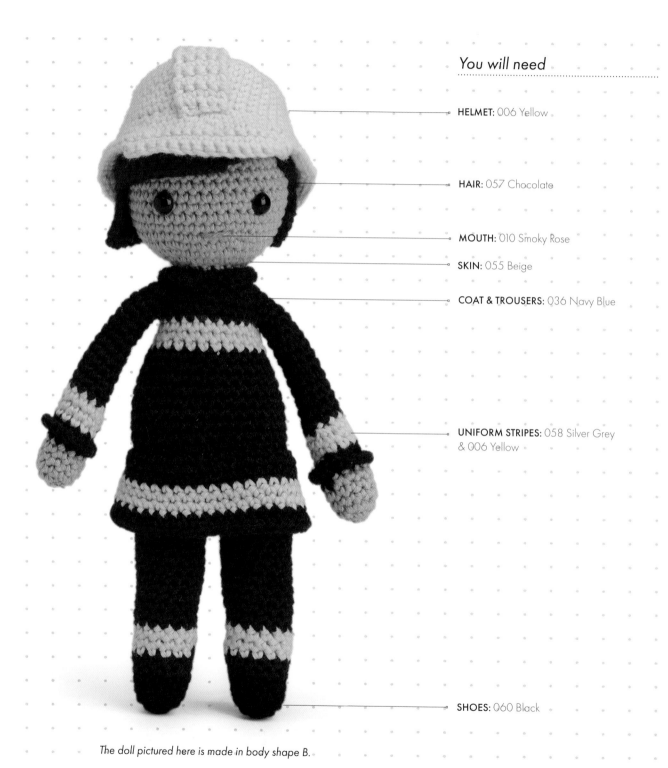

You will need

HELMET: 006 Yellow

HAIR: 057 Chocolate

MOUTH: 010 Smoky Rose

SKIN: 055 Beige

COAT & TROUSERS: 036 Navy Blue

UNIFORM STRIPES: 058 Silver Grey & 006 Yellow

SHOES: 060 Black

The doll pictured here is made in body shape B.

Firefighter

This firefighter is excited to start her training. She has learnt it's not all about fighting fires, but also fire prevention, rescues and fitness training. The real buzz is saving people's lives and knowing you are making a difference.

Crochet each part below in order, referring to the body shape you are making (see pages 16–23).

Body shape A

ARMS
As basic pattern apart from:
Round 8: Work in Yellow.
Round 9: Work in Light Grey.
Round 10: Work in Yellow.
Round 25: Work 2 dc (not 3 dc).

CUFFS
As basic pattern.

LEGS
As basic pattern apart from:
Round 8: Work in Yellow.
Round 9: Work in Light Grey.
Round 10: Work in Yellow.
Round 26: Work 3 dc (not 4 dc).

BODY & HEAD
As basic pattern apart from:
Round 20: Work in Yellow.
Round 21: Work in Light Grey.
Round 22: Work in Yellow.

COLLAR
As basic pattern.

Body shape B

ARMS
As basic pattern apart from:
Round 8: Work in Yellow.
Round 9: Work in Light Grey.
Round 10: Work in Yellow.
Round 22: Work 2 dc (not 3 dc).

CUFFS
As basic pattern.

LEGS
As basic pattern apart from:
Round 8: Work in Yellow.
Round 9: Work in Light Grey.
Round 10: Work in Yellow.
Round 22: Work 5 dc (not 6 dc).

BODY & HEAD
As basic pattern apart from:
Round 17: Work in Yellow.
Round 18: Work in Light Grey.
Round 19: Work in Yellow.

COLLAR
As basic pattern.

Body shape C

ARMS
As basic pattern apart from:
Round 8: Work in Yellow.
Round 9: Work in Light Grey.
Round 10: Work in Yellow.
Round 19: Work 1 dc (not 2 dc).

CUFFS
As basic pattern.

LEGS
As basic pattern apart from:
Round 8: Work in Yellow.
Round 9: Work in Light Grey.
Round 10: Work in Yellow.
Round 19: Work 2 dc (not 3 dc).

BODY & HEAD
As basic pattern apart from:
Round 13: Work in Yellow.
Round 14: Work in Light Grey.
Round 15: Work in Yellow.

COLLAR
As basic pattern.

Bottom of coat

Round 1: Hold doll upside and join Navy Blue to one of the FL left in Round 7 at the back, ch1, dc in each st around with 2 increases, one on each side of the doll.
Round 2: Dc in each st around.
Round 3: Dc in each st around with 2 increases, one on each side of the doll. Change to Yellow.
Round 4: Dc in each st around. Change to Silver Grey.
Round 5: Dc in each st around with 2 increases, one on each side of the doll. Change to Yellow.
Round 6: Dc in each st around. Change to Navy Blue.
Round 7: Dc in each st around with 2 increases, one on each side of the doll.
Round 8: Dc in each st around.
Fasten off and weave in ends.

Hair

Make Longer Bob on page 26 in Chocolate.

Helmet

Round 1: Using Yellow, work into a magic ring, 6 dc.
Round 2: 2 dc in each st to end. (12 sts)
Round 3: (2 dc in next st, 1 dc) 6 times. (18 sts)
Round 4: (2 dc in next st, 2 dc) 6 times. (24 sts)
Round 5: (2 dc in next st, 3 dc) 6 times. (30 sts)
Round 6: (2 dc in next st, 4 dc) 6 times. (36 sts)
Round 7: (2 dc in next st, 5 dc) 6 times. (42 sts)
Rounds 8–14: Dc in each st around.
Round 15: (2 dc in next st, 6 dc) 6 times in FLO. (48 sts)
Round 16: 4 dc, (2 dc in next st, 7 dc) 5 times, 2 dc in next st, 3 dc. (54 sts)
Round 17: (2 dc in next st, 8 dc) 6 times. (60 sts)
Round 18: 5 dc, (2 dc in next st, 9 dc) 5 times, 2 dc in next st, 4 dc. (66 sts)
Now continue in rows to make the brim:
Row 19: Turn, skip 1st st, 17 dc. (17 sts)
Row 20: Turn, skip 1st st, 16 dc. (16 sts)
Row 21: Turn, skip 1st st, sl st, 13 dc, sl st. (15 sts)
Fasten off and weave in end.

HELMET RIDGE
Row 1: Ch5 in Yellow.
Row 2: Dc in 2nd from hook, dc to end, turn. (4 sts)
Rows 3–30: Ch1, dc to end, turn.
Adjust number of rows above to fit the helmet from front to back. Fasten off leaving a tail for sewing. Sew ridge in place.

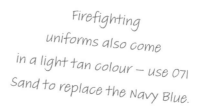

Firefighting uniforms also come in a light tan colour – use 071 Sand to replace the Navy Blue.

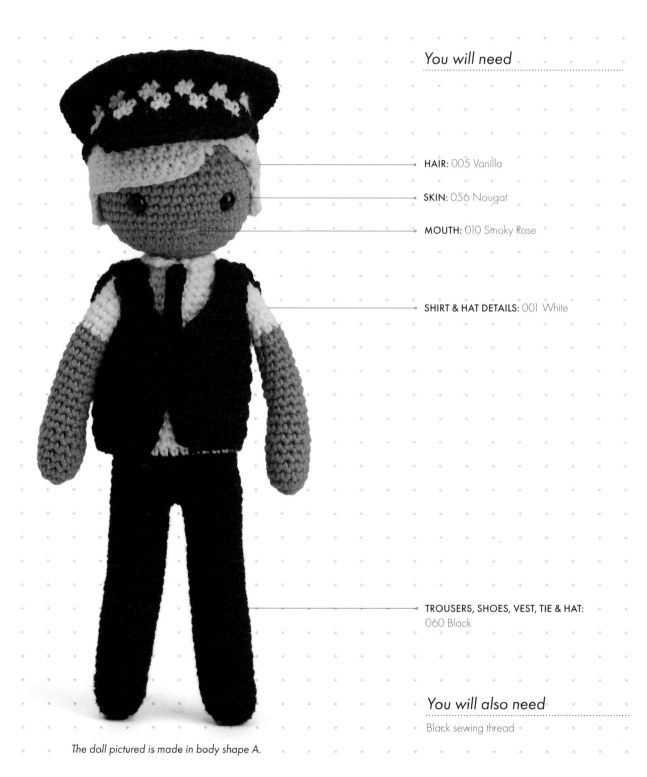

HAIR: 005 Vanilla

SKIN: 056 Nougat

MOUTH: 010 Smoky Rose

SHIRT & HAT DETAILS: 001 White

TROUSERS, SHOES, VEST, TIE & HAT:
060 Black

You will also need

Black sewing thread

The doll pictured is made in body shape A.

Police officer

Being a police officer is primarily about protecting lives, and this is what inspired this officer to join the force. No two days are the same, which is what makes the job so exciting. She particularly enjoys the days when she's out and about meeting people in the community.

Crochet each part below in order, referring to the body shape you are making (see pages 16–23).

Body shape A

ARMS
As basic pattern apart from:
Rounds 1–18: Work in Skin colour.
(Do not work in BLO in round 7.)
Rounds 19–25: Work in White.
Round 25: 2 dc, sl st, leave the remaining sts unworked.

LEGS
As basic pattern apart from:
Work all rounds in Black.

BODY & HEAD
As basic pattern apart from:
Round 8: Do not work in BLO.

Body shape B

ARMS
As basic pattern apart from:
Rounds 1–16: Work in Skin colour.
(Do not work in BLO in round 7.)
Rounds 17–22: Work in White.
Round 22: 2 dc, sl st, leave the remaining sts unworked.

LEGS
As basic pattern apart from:
Work all rounds in Black.

BODY & HEAD
As basic pattern apart from:
Round 8: Do not work in BLO.

Body shape C

ARMS
As basic pattern apart from:
Rounds 1–14: Work in Skin colour.
(Do not work in BLO in round 7.)
Rounds 15–19: Work in White.

LEGS
As basic pattern apart from:
Work all rounds in Black.

BODY & HEAD
As basic pattern apart from:
Round 8: Do not work in BLO.

Vest (body shape A)

Row 1: Ch39 in Black, dc in 2nd ch from hook, dc to end of ch, turn. (38 sts)
Rows 2–12: Ch1, dc across, turn. (38 sts)
Row 13: Ch1, dc2tog, 34 dc, dc2tog, turn. (36 sts)
Row 14: Ch1, dc2tog, 32 dc, dc2tog, turn. (34 sts)
Row 15: Ch1, dc2tog, 3 dc, leave remaining sts unworked, turn. (4 sts)
Row 16: Ch1, 3 dc, leave remaining st unworked, turn. (3 sts)
Rows 17–20: Ch1, 3 dc, turn. (3 sts)
Fasten off. Join yarn in 4th stitch on main panel from strap just made.

Rows 1–4: Ch1, 18 dc, turn. (18 sts)
Row 5: Ch1, dc2tog, 14 dc, dc2tog, turn. (16 sts)
Row 6: Ch1, dc2tog, 12 dc, dc2tog. (14 sts)
Fasten off. Join yarn in last st on main panel.

Row 1: Ch1, dc2tog, 3 dc, leave remaining sts unworked, turn. (4 sts)
Row 2: Ch1, 3 dc, leave remaining st unworked, turn. (3 sts)
Rows 3–6: Ch1, 3 dc, turn. (3 sts)
Fasten off.

Block (see box on facing page) then fold the side panels in and sew the top of the straps to the top of the corners of the back panel. You can leave it open, so it is removable, or sew the edges together to secure in place.

Hair

Make Bob on page 26 in Vanilla.

Vest (body shape B)

Row 1: Ch43 in Black, dc in 2nd ch from hook, dc to end of ch, turn. (42 sts)
Rows 2–9: Ch1, dc across, turn. (42 sts)
Row 10: Ch1, dc2tog, 38 dc, dc2tog, turn. (40 sts)
Row 11: Ch1, dc2tog, 36 dc, dc2tog, turn. (38 sts)
Row 12: Ch1, dc2tog, 3 dc, leave remaining sts unworked, turn. (4 sts)
Row 13: Ch1, 3 dc, leave remaining st unworked, turn. (3 sts)
Rows 14–17: Ch1, 3 dc, turn. (3 sts)
Fasten off. Join yarn in 5th stitch on main panel from strap just made.

Rows 1–4: Ch1, 20 dc, turn. (20 sts)
Row 5: Ch1, dc2tog, 16 dc, dc2tog, turn. (18 sts)
Row 6: Ch1, dc2tog, 14 dc, dc2tog. (16 sts)
Fasten off. Join yarn in last st on main panel.

Row 1: Ch1, dc2tog, 3 dc, leave remaining sts unworked, turn. (4 sts)
Row 2: Ch1, 3 dc, leave remaining st unworked, turn. (3 sts)
Rows 3–6: Ch1, 3 dc, turn. (3 sts)
Fasten off.

Block (see box below) then fold the side panels in and sew the top of the straps to the top of the corners of the back panel. You can leave it open, so it is removable, or sew the edges together to secure in place.

Vest (body shape C)

Row 1: Ch35 in Black, dc in 2nd ch from hook, dc to end of ch, turn. (34 sts)
Rows 2–9: Ch1, dc across, turn. (34 sts)
Row 10: Ch1, dc2tog, 30 dc, dc2tog, turn. (32 sts)
Row 11: Ch1, dc2tog, 28 dc, dc2tog, turn. (30 sts)
Row 12: Ch1, dc2tog, 3 dc, leave remaining sts unworked, turn. (4 sts)
Row 13: Ch1, 3 dc, leave remaining st unworked, turn. (3 sts)
Rows 14–16: Ch1, 3 dc, turn. (3 sts)
Fasten off. Join yarn in 3rd stitch on main panel from strap just made.

Rows 1–3: Ch1, 16 dc, turn. (16 sts)
Row 4: Ch1, dc2tog, 12 dc, dc2tog, turn. (14 sts)
Row 5: Ch1, dc2tog, 10 dc, dc2tog. (12 sts)
Fasten off. Join yarn in last st on main panel.

Row 1: Ch1, dc2tog, 3 dc, leave remaining sts unworked, turn. (4 sts).
Row 2: Ch1, 3 dc, leave remaining st unworked, turn. (3 sts)
Rows 3–5: Ch1, 3 dc, turn. (3 sts)
Fasten off.

Block (see box below) then fold the side panels in and sew the top of the straps to the top of the corners of the back panel. You can leave it open, so it is removable, or sew the edges together to secure in place.

Blocking
This is recommended before sewing. Use a foam blocking board or a folded towel to pin the pieces down. Spray with water then allow to dry overnight. This should stop the corners curling up so much.

Hat

Round 1: Using Black, work into a magic ring, 6 dc.
Round 2: 2 dc in each st to end. (12 sts)
Round 3: (2 dc in next st, 1 dc) 6 times. (18 sts)
Round 4: (2 dc in next st, 2 dc) 6 times. (24 sts)
Round 5: (2 dc in next st, 3 dc) 6 times. (30 sts)
Round 6: (2 dc in next st, 4 dc) 6 times. (36 sts)
Round 7: (2 dc in next st, 5 dc) 6 times. (42 sts)
Round 8: (2 dc in next st, 6 dc) 6 times. (48 sts)
Round 9: (2 dc in next st, 7 dc) 6 times. (54 sts)
Round 10: (2 dc in next st, 8 dc) 6 times. (60 sts)
Round 11: (2 dc in next st, 9 dc) 6 times. (66 sts)
Round 12: Dc in each st around. (66 sts)
Round 13: (Dc2tog, 9 dc) 6 times. (60 sts)
Round 14: (Dc2tog, 8 dc) 6 times. (54 sts)
Round 15: (Dc2tog, 7 dc) 6 times. (48 sts)
Rounds 16–17: Dc in each st around alternating between Black and White every two stitches. Make sure you change colour at the end of the second st to the new colour (see page 11 for colour changing tips). (48 sts)

Round 18: You should have finished the last round on two White sts, do not change colour, make the next 2 dc in White, dc in each st around continuing the pattern.
Round 19: Dc in each st around following the pattern. (48 sts)
Round 20: Dc around in Black. (48 sts)
Now continue in rows to make the brim:
Row 21: Turn, skip first st, in BLO 17 dc, leave rem sts unworked. (17 sts)
Row 22: Turn, skip first st, 16 dc. (16 sts)
Row 23: Turn, skip first st, 15 dc. (15 sts)
Row 24: Turn, skip first st, dc2tog, 2 htr, 2 tr, 2 tr in next st, 2 tr, 2 htr, dc2tog, sl st. (13 sts)
Fasten off and weave in ends.
The hat will perch on the top of the head, but you can sew it into place with black sewing thread if desired.

Tie

Row 1: Ch18 (or however many to reach from the collar to the bottom of the shirt), sl st in 2nd ch from hook, dc in each st to end, fasten off leaving a long tail.
Weave in the starting tail then use the remaining tail to wrap around the top of the tie several times (use a needle to secure it every so often). Use the remaining tail to sew the tie to the neck. Use black sewing thread to sew the bottom on the tie in place.

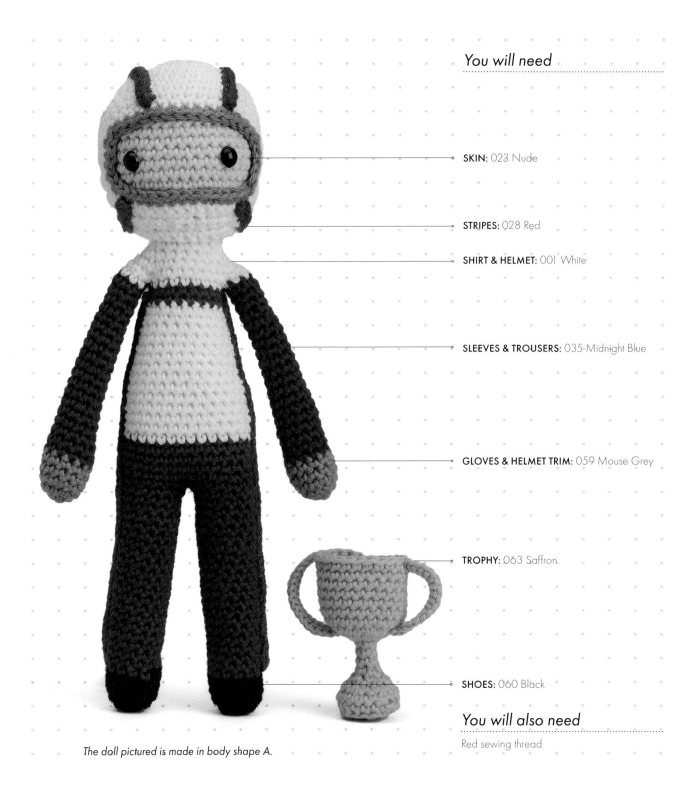

SKIN: 023 Nude

STRIPES: 028 Red

SHIRT & HELMET: 001 White

SLEEVES & TROUSERS: 035 Midnight Blue

GLOVES & HELMET TRIM: 059 Mouse Grey

TROPHY: 063 Saffron

SHOES: 060 Black

You will also need

Red sewing thread

The doll pictured is made in body shape A.

Racing driver

A thrill-seeking personality is key to becoming a racing driver; that, good reflexes and a commitment to training hard. Today this racing driver is competing in the Grand Prix on his home turf, Silverstone in the UK.

Crochet each part below in order, referring to the body shape you are making (see pages 16–23).

Body shape A

ARMS
As basic pattern apart from:
Rounds 1–5: Work in Mouse Grey.
Round 7: Do not work in BLO.
Rounds 8–25: Work in Midnight Blue.

LEGS
As basic pattern.

BODY & HEAD
As basic pattern apart from:
Round 8: Do not work in BLO.
Rounds 21–22: Work in Red.
Rounds 28–29: Work in White, do not work in BLO in round 28, change to Skin colour at the end of round 29.
Do not add stitch for mouth.

Body shape B

ARMS
As basic pattern apart from:
Rounds 1–5: Work in Mouse Grey.
Round 7: Do not work in BLO.
Rounds 8–22: Work in Midnight Blue.

LEGS
As basic pattern.

BODY & HEAD
As basic pattern apart from:
Round 8: Do not work in BLO.
Rounds 18–19: Work in Red.
Rounds 25–26: Work in White, do not work in BLO in round 25, change to Skin colour at the end of round 26.
Do not add stitch for mouth.

Body shape C

ARMS
As basic pattern apart from:
Rounds 1–5: Work in Mouse Grey.
Round 7: Do not work in BLO.
Rounds 8–19: Work in Midnight Blue.

LEGS
As basic pattern.

BODY & HEAD
As basic pattern apart from:
Round 8: Do not work in BLO.
Rounds 14–15: Work in Red.
Rounds 21–22: Work in White, do not work in BLO in round 21, change to Skin colour at the end of round 22.
Do not add stitch for mouth.

RACING SUIT STRIPES (OPTIONAL)
Make 2

Ch48 in Red. (Adjust length for different body shapes.) Sl st in 2nd ch from hook and in each st to end.

Fasten off. Use a similar colour sewing thread and sew the stripes to the body on either side.

Note: The initial ch may have to be longer than necessary as the sl sts tend to shorten it.

Helmet

Round 1: Using White, work into a magic ring, 6 dc. (6 sts)

Round 2: 2 dc in each st to end. (12 sts)

Round 3: (2 dc in next st, 1 dc) 6 times. (18 sts)

Round 4: (2 dc in next st, 2 dc) 6 times. (24 sts)

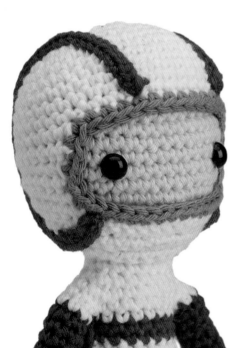

Round 5: (2 dc in next st, 3 dc) 6 times. (30 sts)

Round 6: (2 dc in next st, 4 dc) 6 times. (36 sts)

Round 7: (2 dc in next st, 5 dc) 6 times. (42 sts)

Rounds 8–13: Dc in each st around. (42 sts)

Round 14: Turn, ch1, 28 dc, leave rem sts unworked, turn. (28 sts)

Round 15: Ch1, dc2tog, 24 dc, dc2tog, turn. (26 sts)

Round 16: Ch1, dc in each st to end, turn. (26 sts)

Round 17: Ch1, 2 dc in next st, 24 dc, 2 dc in next st, turn. (28 sts)

Round 18: Ch15, dc in 2nd ch from hook, dc along ch, dc in each st around, turn. (42 sts)

Round 19: Ch1, (dc2tog, 5 dc) 6 times, turn. (36 sts)

Round 20: Ch1, (dc2tog, 4 dc) 6 times, turn. (30 sts)

Round 21: Ch1, (dc2tog, 3 dc) 6 times, turn. (24 sts)

Round 22: Ch1, dc in each st to end, turn. (24 sts)

Fasten off, leaving a long tail for sewing.
You should now have a helmet shape with a flap for the lower part that isn't joined on the right-hand side (left if you are left-handed). With the front of the helmet facing you and the right way up, join Mouse Grey in the far right (left) st on the top edge of the flap. Dc in each st along the edge of the flap and continue up the side, along the top edge and then down the other side. Stop when you are in line to where you started. Place the helmet on the head of the doll. Sl st into the first dc to join. Fasten off and weave in ends. Use the tail end from the helmet to sew the flap to the main part of the helmet using a mattress st (see page 15).

HELMET STRIPES (OPTIONAL)
Make 2

Ch45 in Red. Sl st in 2nd ch from hook and in each st to end.

Fasten off. Use a similar colour sewing thread and sew the stripes onto the helmet.

Note: The initial ch may have to be longer than necessary as the sl sts tend to shorten it.

Trophy

Round 1: Using Saffron, work into a magic ring, 6 dc.

Round 2: 2 dc in each st to end. (12 sts)

Round 3: (2 dc in next st, 1 dc) 6 times. (18 sts)

Round 4: In BLO dc in each st around. (18 sts)

Round 5: Dc in each st around.

Round 6: (Dc2tog, 1dc) 6 times. (12 sts)
Stuff the base with a little stuffing.

Round 7: (Dc2tog) 6 times. (6 sts)

Rounds 8–11: Dc in each st around. (6 sts)

Round 12: 2 dc in each st around. (12 sts)

Round 13: (2 dc in next st, 1dc) 6 times. (18 sts)

Round 14: (2 dc in next st, 2 dc) 6 times. (24 sts)

Rounds 15–21: Dc in each st around. (24 sts)

Sl st to close the spiral. Fasten off and weave in end.

TROPHY HANDLES
Make 2

Ch16 in Saffron. Sl st in 2nd ch from hook and in each st to end.

Fasten off.

Sew each end of the handle to the trophy, repeat with the other handle.

Variations

Here are just a few ways you can customize the dolls.
In fact, there are over 100,000 options, so let your imagination run!

Swap the ponytail for
a hair cap to make a boy
footballer instead of a girl.

Follow one of the body
patterns using any
colours you like to create
a unique doll.

Student
Use the Farmer's
body with the
Singer's hair and the
Teacher's bag.

Designer/Architect
Use the Builder's body with short hair using 058 Silver Grey, and the Teacher's bag and glasses.

Explorer/Archaeologist
Use the Explorer's body and backpack with the Farmer's hair and hat. You could also make the hat in dark brown to match the backpack.

Change the hairstyle and clothing colour to create different looks for the Singer.

Abbreviations and conversions

BL	back loop
BLO	back loop only
ch	chain
dc	double crochet
dc2tog	decrease (dc 2 together)
dtr	double treble crochet
FL	Front loop
FLO	Front loop only
htr	half treble crochet
pm	place (stitch) marker
rem	remaining
rep	repeat
rnd	round
RS	right side
sl st	slip stitch
st(s)	stitch (stitches)
tr	treble crochet
WS	wrong side
yo	yarn over (hook)

UK/US CROCHET TERMS

UK	US
Double crochet	Single crochet
Half treble	Half double crochet
Treble	Double crochet
Double treble	Treble

Note: This book uses UK crochet terms

STANDARD CROCHET HOOKS

UK	METRIC	US
14	2mm	–
13	2.25mm	B/1
12	2.5mm	–
–	2.75mm	C/2
11	3mm	–
10	3.25mm	D/3
9	3.5mm	E/4
–	3.75mm	F/5
8	4mm	G/6
7	4.5mm	7
6	5mm	H/8
5	5.5mm	I/9
4	6mm	J/10
3	6.5mm	K/10.5
2	7mm	–
0	8mm	L/11
00	9mm	M–N/13
000	10mm	N–P/15

Suppliers

In addition to Amazon, which stocks all the tools and materials required for the projects, the following suppliers are recommended.

YARN

Stockists of Ricorumi yarn, offering worldwide shipping.

www.blacksheepwools.com
www.deramores.com
www.ethelandem.com
www.fredaldous.co.uk
www.lovecrafts.com
www.woolwarehouse.co.uk

SAFETY EYES AND SOFT TOY MAKING

UK
www.craftbits.co.uk
www.celloexpress.co.uk

US
www.6060eyes.com

About the author

Kate is a crochet pattern designer based by the sea in Sussex, in the south-east of England. Her love for craft and making things has always been present, and while working as a retail interior designer she started making sock monsters and attending craft fairs in her spare time. As a designer at heart, her business soon evolved into designing sock monster patterns so people could make their own.

When pregnant in 2011 with her first child she came down with a really bad case of flu, but this actually had an upside – she was finally able to sit and learn what she'd always wanted to learn, which was crochet. She fell in love with it immediately. After several blankets she branched out into soft toys for her two children and soon after was designing her own patterns. Since then, she has written many patterns for magazines and yarn companies, and has also appeared on the television series *Kirstie's Handmade Christmas*.

ACKNOWLEDGEMENTS
It has been so much fun to work on this book and to imagine the personalities of all the dolls. I would like to thank Jonathan Bailey for the opportunity to bring these creations to life, and also thank you to Dominique Page for all the hard work and enthusiasm. A huge thanks to my husband Martin for being forever supportive in my creative endeavours and to my two children, Dylan and Freya, who give me inspiration, suggestions and their understanding that they can't play with the dolls (yet).

Index

First published 2021 by
**Guild of Master
Craftsman Publications Ltd**,
Castle Place,
166 High Street,
Lewes,
East Sussex
BN7 1XU, UK

Publisher: Jonathan Bailey
Production: Jim Bulley
Senior Project Editor: Dominique Page
Pattern Checker: Jude Roust
Designer: Sarah Howerd
Photographer: Photography Firm
Illustrators: Robin Shields & Lauren Bergstrom

Colour origination by **GMC Reprographics**
Printed and bound in China

To place an order, contact:

GMC Publications

166 High Street,
Lewes, East Sussex,
BN7 1XU, United Kingdom

+44 (0)1273 488005

www.gmcbooks.com